Make It Now, Bake It Later!

The Next Generation

D1122648

Make It Now, Bake It Later!

The Next Generation

More than 200 Easy and Delicious
Recipes for Make-Ahead Dishes

Ann and Scott Goodfellow

Stewart, Tabori & Chang
New York

Published in 2004 by
Stewart, Tabori & Chang
A Company of La Martinière Groupe
115 West 18th Street
New York, NY 10011

Export Sales to all countries except Canada,
France, and French-speaking Switzerland:
Thames and Hudson Ltd.
181A High Holborn
London WC1V 7QX
England

Canadian Distribution:
Canadian Manda Group
One Atlantic Avenue, Suite 105
Toronto, Ontario M6K 3E7
Canada

Library of Congress Cataloging-in-Publication Data
Goodfellow, Ann, 1948–
    Make it now, bake it later! : the next generation : more than 200 easy and delicious
    recipes for make-ahead dishes / Ann and Scott Goodfellow.
       p.   cm.
    Includes index.
    ISBN: 1-58479-351-1
      1. Make-ahead cookery. 2. Quick and easy cookery. I. Goodfellow, Scott, 1947–
    II. Title.
    TX652.G662 2004
    641.5'55—dc22   2003067276

Designed by Laura Lindgren

The text of this book was composed in Mrs. Eaves, Modern, Bliss, and Romany Script.

Printed in Singapore
10 9 8 7 6 5 4 3 2 1
First Printing

To our daughters,

Allison and Amy,

and the generations to come

Contents

Acknowledgments

We want to offer our special thanks to our wonderfully upbeat editor at Stewart, Tabori & Chang, Jennifer Lang, for her guidance and energy; to our astoundingly efficient recipe editor, Katherine Epstein; and to our superb literary agent, Arielle Eckstut. Thanks to our innovative copyeditor, Sarah Scheffel, and to our designer, Laura Lindgren, for the artistic flair that has brought these pages to life. In a broader sense, we are deeply grateful to our mothers for instilling so much more than good cooking skills in us. They showed us how to open our homes to others and to extend warm, genuine hospitality and individual consideration to every guest.

Further, we would like to offer our sincere thanks and love to all the members of our family and our many good friends who over the years have shared their recipes and ideas with us. Many of the recipes we offer in this book have come through them, and have greatly enriched our family life as well as our entertaining.

Make It Now, Bake It Later! is about much more than a method of food preparation. It represents a concerted effort to free the cook from the kitchen in order to pay complete attention to the interests and enjoyment of family and friends. We gratefully thank all who assisted us in our efforts to share this approach to the art of giving.

Introduction

In 1958, Barbara Goodfellow (Scott's mother) self-published her first
Make It Now, Bake It Later! cookbook in an effort to raise money to fight cystic
fibrosis, a disease that held her goddaughter in its untimely terminal grip.
As a navy officer's wife based in Alexandria, Virginia, Mother had
meticulously planned and tested her recipes over time, serving them to
hundreds of dinner guests. She thought her strengths in cooking could not
only help people suffering from CF, but hosts and hostesses across the
country who spent too much of their entertaining time in the kitchen, and
not enough time mingling with family and guests. Mother had five hundred
copies of the book printed at her own expense. When the finished books
arrived in several shipping boxes, they took up most of the space in the
front hall. The next step was daunting, and Mother said, "Well, at least we
have Christmas gifts taken care of!"

She began a relentless tour of gift shops, bookstores, and department
stores in nearby Washington, D.C. Happily, the book caught on quickly.
The concept struck a cord so Mother branched out, using sales agents
across the country to place the book, all the while handling the "back office
paperwork" from her manual typewriter in the family room. Funds were
raised to help fight cystic fibrosis, and the scores of hosts and hostesses who
relied on the ingenious make-ahead recipes benefited enormously. Mother
wrote six different *Make It Now, Bake It Later!* cookbooks over time, and
ultimately used national publishers to get them into kitchens across the
country. Amazingly, we continue to get requests for the recipes all the time,
even though the books have been out of print for many years. That is what
prompted us to revive the *Make It Now, Bake It Later!* phenomenon: to provide
simple, delicious, and crowd-pleasing recipes to anybody struggling to
balance work, family, and entertaining.

This book is a labor of love. We believe that Mother's powerful idea is
perfect for today's time-is-precious world. Why should friends, family, and

guests all have a great time in the other room while you're stuck in the kitchen? Why can't you just make something easy and delicious ahead of time and cook it right before serving, or pull it out of the refrigerator and serve it after some extra preparation? What piece of mind! What savings of time! *Make It Now, Bake It Later! The Next Generation* takes her ideas one step further. After countless recipe requests, we know which of the original dishes are most popular. As you go through our cookbook, you'll see that we have put a symbol ✳ next to the titles of recipes that come from the original books and have proven their value across decades. We've also included previously unpublished recipes from Mother's private collection, and we've added many new ones that have grown to great popularity at our home. Each recipe tells you which ingredients you'll need now and when you'll need additional ingredients later, and exactly when to stop and store the dish until you're ready to serve. We'll let you know whether to put it in the refrigerator or freezer, how long you can leave it there, and what final steps need to be taken before serving. This could mean putting the dish in the oven, tossing salad ingredients, or simply bringing the dish to room temperature. Your guests will barely know you've done anything and—*voilà!*— your entire meal is served. You can even plan (and make) an entire week's worth of meals in advance!

We invite you to step out of today's high-pressure whirlwind of a world and enjoy your family and friends and the passion of cooking for them. Our belief is that you, as host or hostess, are the key to the success of any meal, party, luncheon, or festive occasion. And if you plan carefully, you can make this an *easy* burden to bear, with a guarantee of success! The recipes and ideas in *Make It Now, Bake It Later!* will make both everyday family life and entertaining easy—and all you need to do is plan ahead. We cannot overestimate the self-confidence and pride that this simple approach will give you. Join us in the pleasure of entertaining at home.

Just a moment—is that the doorbell we hear?

Starters

$\mathcal{A}$ny guest you entertain will look at the starters you're serving and immediately jump to conclusions about what the rest of the meal will be like. As in most of life, first impressions are key! Knowing this secret to a great dinner or party is half the battle.

The *Make It Now, Bake It Later!* approach requires only that you plan ahead. Good planning and lots of make-ahead dishes will ensure that you enjoy your party as much as your guests. For one thing, serve a variety of starters—never make fewer than two. We've found that this is the best way to start a buzz in the room and get people into party mode. And be sure all the starters are different—hot and cold, meat and vegetable, bite-sized tidbits and spreads overflowing with cheese and fruit. You can serve individual starters such as Ping-Pong Sausage Balls (page 57) along with a Lost City of Gold Cheesecake (page 34) arranged on a platter with a variety of crackers. Inventive, fabulous starters will launch any party with unabashed enthusiasm. Planning ahead makes it all work, and if your starters are well-received, you'll know that the rest of your meal will be greeted with anticipation.

Some people think that appetizers are there to stave off hunger while you're waiting for the main course. Banish the thought! While the main course is very important, it's the starters that set the stage for the entire meal. Decide early on what these morsels will be and then present them with flair. Everything that follows will improve magically under the halo of your delicious first impression.

Burgundy Mushrooms

This is our most requested recipe. You'll find it's worth the price of the book when your guests eat every last one! If you do end up with leftovers, these mushrooms are great as a side dish with steaks and other main courses.

4 pounds whole fresh mushrooms (the smaller, the better)
1 cup margarine (2 sticks)
1 cup butter (2 sticks)
1 quart red Burgundy wine (cheap wine will do)
2 tablespoons Worcestershire sauce
1 teaspoon dill seed
1 teaspoon freshly ground black pepper
1 teaspoon garlic powder
2 cups boiling water
4 beef bouillon cubes
4 chicken bouillon cubes

NOW

Wash the mushrooms; remove and discard the stems. If the caps are too large, cut them into bite-sized pieces.

Put all the ingredients in a large pot, and bring them to a rapid boil over high heat. Reduce heat to low, cover, and simmer for 5 to 6 hours. Stir occasionally. (At this point, you can stop, cool, and refrigerate until you're ready to continue cooking.) Uncover them and simmer for 3 to 5 hours more, stirring occasionally, until the mushrooms look like pebbles in a brook. The liquid will reduce somewhat but will not thicken. Remove from heat, and let cool.

Cover and refrigerate for up to 3 days, or freeze. If you are freezing the mushrooms, then transfer them, along with their liquid, to an airtight container. (If you use more than one container, make sure to divide the liquid equally among the containers.) Freeze for up to 3 months.

LATER

If refrigerated, reheat the mushrooms and their liquid in a large saucepan over low heat until thoroughly warmed, about 25 minutes. Drain the mushrooms, reserving the liquid in case there are any leftovers.

If frozen, remove the mushrooms from the freezer, and slowly warm as described above. It will take about 45 minutes.

Serve warm, with toothpicks.

TIP The above cooking periods can be done over 1 or 2 days. To wash mushrooms: Fill the sink half full with warm water and add about $1/2$ cup salt. Stir the water to dissolve the salt and add the mushrooms. Swirl the mushrooms around, and you'll be amazed at how clean they become—in record time.

Serves 20

Pickles in a Blanket

These simple, yet unique starters are our daughter Allison's pièce de résistance and one of the most popular appetizers our family has to offer. Your guests will be hoping to see them on their next visit!

1 cup cream cheese (8 ounces), softened

12 ounces thinly sliced boiled ham

One 32-ounce jar refrigerated whole dill pickles, drained and put on paper
    towels to dry (Claussen are our favorite)

NOW

Spread the cream cheese over one side of each ham slice, making sure you spread to the edges. Lay a pickle on top, at one end of the ham slice, and roll it up. Repeat until you have run out of ham slices. Place the rolls seam side down on a cookie sheet, cover with plastic wrap, and refrigerate overnight or up to 2 days.

LATER

Slice each roll into ¼-inch-thick slices. Arrange on a serving platter, and refrigerate until serving time.

Makes about 30 slices

✳ Our Favorite "Chip 'n' Dip" Dip

Simple, yet delicious—everyone will think there's a secret to it.

NOW

1 tablespoon beef bouillon granules
3 to 4 tablespoons boiling water
1 cup cream cheese (8 ounces)
$1/4$ cup mayonnaise, or more if needed
5 green onions (scallions), finely chopped
$1/2$ teaspoon Beau Monde seasoning

LATER

Potato chips or fresh vegetables, for dipping

NOW

In a serving bowl, dissolve bouillon granules in the boiling water. Using an electric beater, beat the cream cheese with the bouillon broth until well mixed. Stir in the mayonnaise, green onions, and Beau Monde. Cover and refrigerate overnight or up to 1 week.

LATER

Remove from the refrigerator, and let sit at room temperature for about 1 hour to soften. Stir in more mayonnaise, if needed, to achieve your desired dipping consistency. Serve with potato chips or raw vegetables.

Serves 4 to 6

Artichoke Sunburst

A glamorous, delicious appetizer! On the serving platter, the leaves radiate from the center in a beautiful sunburst.

2 large artichokes
1 tablespoon cider vinegar
$^1/_2$ cup plus 1 tablespoon salad oil, divided
1 cup cream cheese (8 ounces), softened
$^1/_4$ teaspoon hot pepper sauce
$^1/_2$ teaspoon garlic powder
1 teaspoon dried dill weed, divided
1 tablespoon red wine vinegar
$^1/_2$ teaspoon dried basil
$^1/_2$ teaspoon dried parsley
$^1/_2$ teaspoon dried thyme
$^1/_2$ teaspoon dried oregano
2 cloves garlic, minced
Freshly ground black pepper
$^1/_2$ pound small shrimp, cleaned, peeled, and cooked

NOW

Cut the stems off the artichokes, making a flat base for them to rest on. Put them in a large pot, stem side down. Add enough water to the pot to cover about two-thirds of the artichokes. Add the cider vinegar and 1 tablespoon of the salad oil to the water. Cover the pot, and bring to a boil over high heat. Reduce heat to low, and simmer for 40 minutes. Drain the artichokes, transfer them to an airtight container, and refrigerate until thoroughly chilled.

In a small bowl, combine the cream cheese, hot pepper sauce, garlic powder, and $^1/_2$ teaspoon of the dill. Cover and refrigerate. In another bowl, whisk together the remaining $^1/_2$ cup salad oil, the red wine vinegar, basil, parsley, thyme, oregano, garlic, and pepper to taste. Add the shrimp, and stir gently until they are completely coated with dressing. Cover and transfer to the refrigerator to marinate at least 2 hours or overnight.

LATER

Remove the artichokes, cream cheese topping, and shrimp mixture from the refrigerator. Drain the shrimp, discarding the liquid, and set them aside. Remove and reserve the artichoke leaves. (You should discard the toughest outer leaves, the tiny inner leaves, and the choke. Save the heart for another purpose.) Put 1 teaspoon of the cream cheese topping inside each leaf, on the tender end. Top each with a small shrimp.

Transfer the leaves to a large, round platter: Starting on the outer edge, arrange the leaves so they point outward in a circular pattern, ending in the center with a small bowl for discarding the scraped leaves. Cover and refrigerate at least 1 hour or up to 6 hours. Serve chilled.

Makes 30 to 40 leaves

Artichoke Bread Cauldron

People simply love a unique dip served in a bread bowl. The presentation can't be beat! This dip is fabulous, but eating the bread it's cooked in (after your guests depart) is even better.

NOW

5 to 6 green onions (scallions), finely chopped

5 cloves garlic, minced

$^1/_2$ cup butter (1 stick)

1 cup cream cheese (8 ounces), softened

2 cups sour cream

One 12-ounce jar marinated artichoke hearts, drained and chopped

2 cups shredded cheddar-jack cheese (or use cheddar or Monterey Jack cheese, or a combination)

LATER

1 round loaf pumpernickel or sourdough bread, unsliced

2 baguettes, sliced

NOW

In a large skillet, sauté the green onions and garlic briefly in the butter. Set aside. Blend the cream cheese and sour cream in a medium bowl until smooth. Add the artichoke hearts, cheese, and green onion mixture, and mix thoroughly. Cover and refrigerate for up to 3 days.

LATER

Preheat a broiler. Carefully cut off (and reserve) the top third of the round loaf, and hollow out the inside, leaving the sides and bottom intact. Place the hollowed-out bread and its top on a baking sheet. Toast under the broiler for about 2 minutes, or until lightly browned. (Watch carefully, it will brown rapidly.)

Preheat the oven to 350°F. Fill the bread with the chilled artichoke dip, and top with the bread "lid." Wrap in aluminum foil and place on a wire rack on a baking sheet. Bake for 1½ hours. Remove the foil, transfer the bread bowl to a serving dish, and serve warm with the baguette slices.

Artichoke Dip

We've tried many versions of this recipe, and this one is our favorite. The green chiles add tang and color, and the simplicity of the recipe is perfect for last-minute guests who call to say they're dropping by. You bake this in 20 minutes and have it ready in time for their arrival.

NOW
1 cup grated Parmesan cheese
1 cup mayonnaise
One 13-ounce can artichoke hearts, drained and chopped
4 ounces canned diced green chiles
1 cup shredded mozzarella cheese (or your favorite cheese)
One 4¼-ounce can chopped ripe olives, optional
1 cup fresh cooked or canned crabmeat or chopped shrimp, optional

LATER
Crackers, for serving

NOW

Mix all the ingredients in a large bowl, and pour them into a greased baking dish. Bake immediately, or cover tightly and refrigerate for up to 1 day.

LATER

Preheat the oven to 400°F. Uncover the dip and bake it for 20 minutes, until bubbly and lightly browned. Serve warm with crackers. (If you have leftover dip to reheat, cover it with plastic wrap and microwave it for 3 minutes.)

Serves 6 to 8

Jacket Asparagus

Dress your asparagus up in jackets, and suddenly they're both elegant and fun.

24 slices white bread, crusts removed
24 spears fresh asparagus, or two 15-ounce cans asparagus (do not use extra long), well drained
1 cup cream cheese (8 ounces), softened
4 ounces blue cheese or Roquefort, crumbled (1 cup)
1 egg, lightly beaten
$^1/_2$ cup butter or margarine (1 stick), melted
$^1/_3$ cup grated Parmesan cheese

NOW

Flatten the bread slices with a rolling pin or the side of a glass. Set aside. If you're using fresh asparagus, remove and discard the tough ends of the asparagus, and peel the stalks with a vegetable peeler. Steam the asparagus for about 4 minutes or until tender-crisp. Drain and set aside to cool.

In a small bowl, blend the cream cheese, blue cheese, and egg. Spread the cheese mixture on one side of each slice of bread. Place a spear of asparagus at one end of each slice of bread, and roll the bread around the asparagus. Roll each cylinder in the melted butter and then in the Parmesan. Cut each cylinder in half, place on a baking sheet, uncovered, and freeze. When the asparagus is frozen, transfer the cylinders to an airtight container, and return them to the freezer for up to 3 months.

LATER

Preheat the oven to 350°F. Spray a baking sheet with vegetable cooking spray. Transfer the frozen asparagus to the baking sheet, and bake them for 15 to 20 minutes, until lightly browned.

Makes 48 pieces

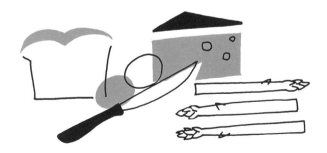

Bacon Bites

With these tasty items, plus Montgomery Square Cocktail Pizzas (page 54), and Mexican Layered Dip (page 45), you have an instant Super Bowl party with virtually no effort at party time!

$^1/_4$ cup butter ($^1/_2$ stick)
1 cup water
2 cups Pepperidge Farm herb seasoned stuffing mix
1 egg, lightly beaten
$^1/_4$ cup finely chopped onion
$^1/_2$ pound sausage meat (hot or mild)
10 slices bacon, cut into thirds

NOW

Place the butter and water in a medium saucepan over medium-high heat, and stir until the butter melts. Remove from heat. Add the stuffing mix, egg, onion, and sausage, and mix thoroughly with your hands. Cover and refrigerate for 1 hour.

Uncover the sausage mixture, and shape into balls the size of walnuts. Wrap each ball with a strip of bacon and secure it with a toothpick. Transfer to baking sheets, and freeze, uncovered. When the balls are frozen, transfer them to an airtight container, and return them to the freezer for up to 3 months.

LATER

Preheat the oven to 375°F. Place the frozen bites in a roasting pan with a rack, and bake for 35 minutes, turning once. Serve hot.

Makes 30 bites

Blue Cheese Roll-Ups

If you have a stash of these how-many-can-you-eat appetizers in the freezer, unexpected company will be amazed at how fast you can present them.

1 cup cream cheese (8 ounces), softened
4 ounces blue cheese, crumbled (1 cup)
$1/2$ cup chopped ripe olives or chopped pimiento-stuffed green olives
18 slices white bread, crusts removed
$1/2$ cup butter (1 stick), melted

NOW

In a small bowl, combine the cheeses and olives, mixing well. Flatten the bread slices using a rolling pin or the side of a glass. Spread one side of each piece of bread with the cream cheese mixture. Then, starting with the long edge, roll the bread and cheese to form a cylinder with the bread on the outside. Roll each cylinder in the melted butter. Cut each cylinder into 3 sections, place the pieces on a baking sheet, and freeze, uncovered. When the roll-ups are frozen, transfer them to an airtight container, and return them to the freezer for up to 3 months.

LATER

Preheat oven to 400°F. Arrange the frozen roll-ups on a baking sheet, and bake them for 15 to 20 minutes, until lightly browned.

TIP You can divide the cheese mixture in half and add $1/4$ cup black olives to one half and $1/4$ cup stuffed green olives to the other half.

Makes 54 roll-ups

French Quarter Cheese

No need to import Boursin cheese from France—you can whip it up in your own kitchen.

NOW
2 cups cream cheese (16 ounces), softened
1 clove garlic, crushed
1 teaspoon whole caraway seeds
1 teaspoon dried basil
1 teaspoon dried dill weed

LATER
Lemon pepper
Crackers, for serving

NOW
Put the cream cheese, garlic, caraway, basil, and dill in a medium bowl, and beat with a mixer on medium speed until smooth. Transfer to a serving dish, cover, and refrigerate for up to 2 weeks.

LATER
Sprinkle lemon pepper to taste on top, and serve with your favorite crackers.

Makes 2 cups dip

Beer Can Races Chili Dip

Perfect for watching squadrons of colorful sailboats compete in the weekly fun-for-all beer can races.

NOW

One 15-ounce can all-meat chili (no beans, please)
1 cup cream cheese (8 ounces), softened
1 package (1¼ ounces) taco seasoning
One 4-ounce can diced green chiles, optional
2 cups grated cheddar-jack cheese (or use cheddar or Monterey Jack
cheese or a combination)

LATER
Tortilla chips, for serving

NOW

Grease a 9- or 10-inch pie pan and set aside. Combine the chili, cream cheese, and taco seasoning until well mixed. Stir in the chiles and grated cheese. Pour the mixture into the prepared pie dish. Cover and refrigerate for up to 3 days.

LATER

Preheat the oven to 350°F. Uncover the chili mixture, and bake for 20 to 30 minutes, until bubbly and heated through. Serve hot, with tortilla chips. (If you have any leftover dip to reheat, cover it with plastic wrap, and microwave for up to 3 minutes, until heated through.)

TIP To make this spicier, use Mexican cheese combined with jalapeños.

Serves 6 to 10

Curry Torte

If you're looking for something with a South Asian twist, these exotic flavors combine for an extraordinary appetizer. This is one of our favorites!

NOW

1 cup low-fat cottage cheese

2 cups cream cheese (16 ounces), softened

2 teaspoons curry powder

One 9-ounce jar mango chutney (be sure it has small-sized chunks), divided

1 cup finely sliced green onions (scallions), divided

1 cup coarsely chopped cocktail peanuts, divided

1 cup golden raisins, divided

1 cup crumbled bacon or bacon bits, divided

1 cup toasted coconut, divided

LATER

Crackers, for serving

NOW

Line a 9 x 5-inch loaf pan with plastic wrap, leaving enough wrap to completely cover the top of the loaf pan. Set aside. Combine the cottage cheese, cream cheese, and curry powder, and blend until smooth.

Gently spread one-half of the cheese mixture over the bottom of the loaf pan. Cover with ½ cup of the chutney, spreading from edge to edge. Then top with ½ cup of the green onions, ½ cup of the peanuts, ½ cup of the raisins, ½ cup of the bacon, and ½ cup of the coconut. Add the remaining

MAKE IT NOW, BAKE IT LATER!

cheese mixture, spreading it to the edges of the pan to seal. Cover tightly with plastic wrap and refrigerate for 8 hours or up to 3 days. Store the remaining garnishes until you are ready to serve the torte.

LATER

Unwrap the plastic wrap and invert the loaf pan onto a serving platter. Gently peel the plastic wrap off the torte. Top the torte with layers of the remaining chutney, green onions, peanuts, raisins, bacon, and toasted coconut. Serve with your favorite crackers.

TIP This torte can be made into two 7 x 4-inch mini loaves. For a spicier version, use Bengal chutney.

Serves 8 to 20

Curried Bites

These are all-purpose, but especially great to serve with soups and salads.

One 4¼-ounce can chopped ripe olives
8 ounces cheddar cheese, grated (2 cups)
3 green onions (scallions), finely chopped
1 cup mayonnaise
1 teaspoon curry powder
6 English muffins, halved

NOW

In a small bowl, combine the olives, cheese, onions, mayonnaise, and curry powder, and mix well. Spread the mixture on the English muffin halves. Cut each muffin half into four wedges. Place the wedges on a baking sheet, cheese side up, and freeze, uncovered. When frozen, transfer the wedges to an airtight container, and return them to the freezer for up to 3 months.

LATER

Preheat oven to 375°F. Transfer the frozen wedges to a baking sheet, and bake for about 20 minutes, until the cheese begins to bubble. Serve warm.

TIP You can omit the olives and add 1 cup fresh or canned crabmeat.

Makes 48 wedges

Park City Pesto Brie

When the Brie is gone, your guests will fight over pieces of the bread bowl!

NOW
1 round loaf sourdough bread, unsliced
1 small round Brie cheese (13 to 15 ounces)
1 cup prepared pesto

LATER
Toasted baguette slices or crackers, for serving

NOW
Preheat the oven to 400°F. Carefully cut off and reserve the top third of the bread round. Hollow out the inside of the loaf, leaving the sides and bottom intact. Place the hollowed-out bread round and its top on a baking sheet, and bake for 10 minutes, until lightly browned. (Watch carefully, it will brown rapidly.) Set the bread aside to cool.

While the bread is cooling, remove and discard the rind from the Brie. Cut the Brie into chunks. (Removing the rind is a matter of taste. This recipe also works if you leave the rind on. We just prefer the taste without it.)

Spread one-half of the pesto on the bottom and sides of the bread bowl to cover. Add the chunks of cheese, and cover with the remaining pesto. Put the top of the loaf back on the bread. Wrap the round in plastic wrap, and refrigerate for 2 to 4 hours

LATER
Remove the plastic, and wrap the bread in two layers of paper towels. Microwave for up to 7 minutes on high. Remove the paper towels and the bread lid. Carefully stir the cheese mixture. If the cheese has not completely melted, then replace the bread lid, wrap with new paper towels, and microwave 3 minutes more. Stir the cheese again. Serve with toasted baguette slices or crackers.

Serves 6 to 10

Marblehead Holiday Cranberry-Glazed Brie

This cheese spread looks absolutely dazzling and tastes great, too. It's a perfect appetizer for the Thanksgiving and Christmas holidays.

NOW

3 cups fresh cranberries

$^3/_4$ cup firmly packed dark brown sugar

$^1/_3$ cup currants

$^1/_3$ cup water

$^1/_4$ teaspoon dry mustard

$^1/_4$ teaspoon ground allspice

$^1/_4$ teaspoon ground cardamom

$^1/_4$ teaspoon ground cloves

$^1/_4$ teaspoon ground ginger

One 12-inch round of Brie cheese

LATER

Crackers or apple and pear slices, for serving

NOW

Combine the cranberries, brown sugar, currants, water, and spices in a heavy non-aluminum saucepan. Cook over medium-high heat until most of the berries pop, stirring frequently, about 5 minutes. Cool to room temperature. Cover and refrigerate for up to 3 days.

Using a sharp knife, cut out a circle of rind from the top of the Brie, leaving a $^1/_2$-inch border of rind. Carefully remove and discard the circle. Transfer the cheese to a pie plate or other oven-safe serving dish. Spread the cranberry mixture on top of the cheese. Cover and refrigerate for 1 to 6 hours.

LATER

Preheat the oven to 325°F. Bring the cheese with the cranberry topping to room temperature. Set the cheese in the oven and bake for about 20 minutes, until softened. Serve with crackers or apple and pear slices.

TIP   To prepare apple and pear slices ahead of time and prevent browning, put the slices in plastic bags. Pour pineapple juice into the bags to cover the fruit and refrigerate. Drain before serving.

Serves 12 to 20

Sacre Bleu! Cheese Ball

A blue cheese–lover's delight.

NOW
1 cup cream cheese (8 ounces), softened
4 ounces blue cheese, crumbled (1 cup)
1 clove garlic, minced
One 4¹/₄-ounce can chopped ripe olives
1 cup finely chopped pecans

LATER
Crackers, for serving

NOW
Allow the cheeses to come to room temperature. Combine them with the garlic, mixing thoroughly. Fold in the olives. Form the cheese mixture into a ball (or 2 balls), and roll it in the chopped pecans. Wrap it securely, and refrigerate for up to 2 weeks.

LATER
Bring to room temperature and serve with crackers.

TIP If you're in a hurry, combine all the ingredients and put the spread in a serving bowl, without forming it into a ball. (When we do it this way, we omit the pecans or simply sprinkle them on top.) Wrap securely, and refrigerate for up to 2 weeks.

Serves 6 to 8

Holiday Pie

Don't tell anyone what's in this pie—let them be surprised! It's one of our favorites; the green and reddish colors make it perfect for winter holidays.

NOW
1 cup cream cheese (8 ounces), softened
1 cup sour cream
One 5-ounce jar dried chipped beef, coarsely chopped
$1/2$ red onion, finely chopped
$1/2$ green bell pepper, finely chopped
Pepper

LATER
Crackers, for serving

NOW
Lightly grease a 9- or 10-inch pie pan, and set aside. Combine all the ingredients, mixing well and spread into the prepared pie dish. Cover and refrigerate for up to 2 days.

LATER
Preheat the oven to 400°F. Uncover and bake the pie for 20 minutes, until lightly browned. Serve warm, with your favorite crackers.

Serves 6 to 8

Lost City of Gold Cheesecake

Your guests will be dazzled by both the taste and beauty of this treat. The fact that it's a cheesecake (that's really a dip) will be as elusive to your guests as the fabled cities of gold were to the Spanish explorers.

NOW

1¹/₂ cups tortilla chips, finely crushed

¹/₄ cup butter (¹/₂ stick), melted

2 cups cream cheese (16 ounces), softened

2 cups shredded cheddar-jack cheese (or use cheddar or Monterey Jack, or
   a combination)

3 eggs

One 4-ounce can diced green chiles

1 package (1¹/₄ ounces) taco seasoning

¹/₂ cup sour cream

1 cup salsa, hot or mild

LATER

1 cup guacamole

1 cup sour cream

1 cup finely diced red or yellow bell pepper

¹/₂ cup sliced green onions (scallions)

1 medium tomato, chopped and drained

One 4 ¹/₄-ounce can sliced black olives

1 cup finely chopped cilantro

Tortilla chips, for serving

NOW

Preheat the oven to 350°F. Combine the tortilla chips and melted butter in a small bowl. Press onto the bottom (but not the sides) of a 9-inch springform pan, and bake for 10 minutes. Set aside, but do not turn off the oven.

In a large bowl or a food processor, beat together the cream cheese, cheese, and eggs until well blended. Add the chiles, taco seasoning, sour cream, and salsa, and mix well. Pour the cheese mixture over the tortilla chip crust and bake for 35 to 45 minutes more, until the center is firm. Remove the cheesecake from the oven and let it cool. Cover tightly and refrigerate for up to 1 week.

LATER

Uncover the cheesecake, and gently run a knife around the edge of the pan. Carefully remove the outer rim of the pan, spread guacamole over the top, and then top with sour cream. Garnish with the peppers, green onions, tomatoes, olives, and cilantro—or anything you like. Serve with additional tortilla chips.

Serves 15

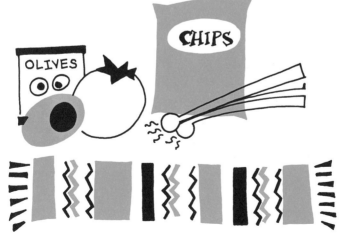

Garlic and Herb Blue Cheesecake

The garlic and herb cheese gives this delectable cheesecake a creamy richness that is unsurpassed.

NOW
1 cup cracker crumbs (from buttery crackers)
2 tablespoons melted butter
4 ounces garlic and herb cheese spread
1½ cups cream cheese (12 ounces), softened
12 ounces Gorgonzola, Stilton, or blue cheese, crumbled (3 cups)
1 cup sour cream
3 eggs
⅛ teaspoon freshly ground black pepper
¼ cup sherry
⅓ cup milk

LATER
½ to 1 cup sour cream, optional
Fresh chopped herbs of your choice, for garnish
Toasted baguette slices, crackers, or fresh fruit, for serving

NOW

Preheat oven to 350°F. Spray a 9-inch springform pan with vegetable spray, and set aside. Combine the cracker crumbs and melted butter, and press into the bottom (but not the sides) of the prepared pan. Bake the crust for 5 to 8 minutes, until lightly browned. Combine the cheeses, sour cream, eggs, pepper, sherry, and milk in a food processor. Pulse until well combined. Pour the cheese mixture onto the crust, smoothing the top with a rubber spatula.

Wrap the bottom and sides of the springform pan with a double thickness of aluminum foil (to help keep the water out), and place the pan inside a larger pan. Add water to the larger pan to come halfway up the sides of the springform pan. Bake for 50 to 55 minutes, but watch carefully to prevent overbaking. (After about 40 minutes, insert a sharp knife into the middle of the cheesecake. The knife will come out clean when the cheesecake is done.) Allow the cheesecake to cool thoroughly. Cover tightly and refrigerate it overnight or up to 1 week.

LATER

Uncover the cheesecake and gently run a knife around the edge of the pan. Carefully remove the outer rim of the pan, and transfer the cheesecake to a serving platter. Decorate the top with sour cream if desired and chopped fresh herbs. Serve with toasted baguette slices, crackers, or slices of fresh fruit (apples and pears both work well).

TIP If the top starts to brown before the cheesecake is finished baking, lay a piece of aluminum foil on top to prevent further browning.

Serves 15 to 20

Piazza Pesto Cheesecake

Piazzas are the neighborhood squares sprinkled throughout the towns and cities of Italy where neighbors meet and socialize. Simple to make, this cheesecake is also delicious!

NOW
1 tablespoon butter, softened
$1/3$ cup plain fine breadcrumbs
$1/2$ cup plus 3 tablespoons freshly grated Parmesan cheese, divided
2 cups cream cheese (16 ounces), softened
1 cup ricotta cheese
$1/4$ teaspoon salt
$1/8$ teaspoon cayenne pepper
3 large eggs
$1/2$ cup prepared pesto
$1/4$ cup pine nuts

LATER
Crackers, for serving

NOW

Preheat the oven to 325°F. Rub the butter over the bottom and sides of a 9-inch springform pan. Mix the breadcrumbs with the 3 tablespoons Parmesan cheese, and coat the bottom and sides of the pan with the mixture. Set aside.

Using an electric mixer, beat the cream cheese, ricotta, remaining $1/2$ cup Parmesan, salt, and cayenne in a large bowl. Add the eggs, one at a time, beating well after each addition. Transfer half of the cheese mixture to another bowl and reserve. Mix the pesto into the remaining half. Pour the pesto mixture into the prepared pan and smooth the top. Carefully spoon the reserved cheese mixture over the top, and gently smooth it. Sprinkle with the pine nuts.

Bake the cheesecake until the center doesn't jiggle when the pan is shaken, about 45 minutes. Transfer the pan to a rack to cool. Cover tightly with plastic wrap, and refrigerate overnight or up to 1 week.

LATER
Uncover the cheesecake and gently run a sharp knife around the edge of the pan. Carefully remove the outer rim of the pan, and transfer the cheesecake to a serving platter. Serve with your favorite crackers.

Serves 15

Josephinas

Josephinas—little bread rounds with tasty toppings—are wonderful all by themselves or with soups and salads. Keep the cheese topping on hand for emergencies—it keeps in the refrigerator for a couple of weeks, so you can use it whenever it's needed.

NOW

One 4-ounce can diced green chiles

$^{1}/_{2}$ cup butter (1 stick), softened

1 clove garlic, crushed

1 cup mayonnaise

2 cups shredded cheddar-jack cheese (or use cheddar or Monterey Jack cheese, or a combination)

LATER

1 baguette, sliced

NOW

In a medium bowl, mix the chiles, butter, garlic, and mayonnaise. Add the cheese and mix until well blended. Cover and refrigerate for up to 2 weeks.

LATER

Preheat oven to 400°F. Lightly spray a baking sheet with vegetable spray, and set aside. Spread the baguette slices generously with the cheese mixture, and place them on the prepared baking sheet. Bake for about 10 minutes, until the cheese spread is bubbly and lightly browned. Serve immediately.

 TIP Many grocery stores will slice the baguette into thin little rounds for you.

Makes about 30 slices

Tuscany Mozzarella

This appetizer looks terrific, especially served in a dark-colored dish.

NOW

$1/4$ cup extra-virgin olive oil

$1/4$ cup vegetable oil

$1/4$ cup bottled sun-dried tomatoes, reserving 1 tablespoon of the oil

$1/2$ teaspoon red pepper flakes

$1/4$ cup fresh parsley leaves

$1/2$ cup fresh basil leaves

$1/4$ cup fresh chives

2 cloves garlic

1 pound whole mozzarella cheese, chilled and sliced $1/4$-inch thick (cut the slices in half if they are too large for the baguette slices)

LATER
1 baguette, sliced

NOW

Combine the oils, sun-dried tomatoes, and reserved oil, red pepper flakes, parsley, basil, chives, and garlic in a food processor, and process until finely chopped. Transfer 1 to 2 tablespoons of the herb mixture to the bottom of a shallow serving dish, and swirl it around. Arrange overlapping slices of the mozzarella in the dish. Spread the remaining herb mixture over the mozzarella slices. Cover and refrigerate for at least 2 hours, but preferably overnight, or up to 5 days.

LATER

Remove the serving dish from the refrigerator 1 hour before serving to allow the mozzarella to return to room temperature. Serve with baguette slices.

TIP   Resist the temptation to add a little more oil: the extra oil will seep out while the mozzarella sits. This cheese is also great on sandwiches and in salads.

Makes about 30 servings

Marvelous Meatballs

These meatballs are a great starter dish, and the leftovers are terrific served over rice as a main course.

NOW
Vegetable oil, for deep frying
2 pounds ground beef
1 cup plain breadcrumbs
$^1/_2$ cup finely chopped almonds
One 5-ounce can water chestnuts, drained and finely chopped
2 eggs
1 tablespoon soy sauce
2 cloves garlic, minced
$^1/_4$ cup cornstarch

LATER
2 tablespoons cornstarch
$^1/_2$ cup white distilled vinegar
$^1/_2$ cup water
1 teaspoon fresh grated ginger
$^3/_4$ cup sugar
$^1/_4$ cup soy sauce
2 teaspoons curry powder
One 15-ounce can unsweetened pineapple chunks, drained

NOW
In a large pot, preheat 1-inch of the vegetable oil for deep frying.

Combine the ground beef, breadcrumbs, almonds, water chestnuts, eggs, soy sauce, and garlic, and mix well. Form into marble-sized balls. Put the cornstarch in a shallow bowl, and roll the meatballs in it, coating them well. When the oil is hot, but not smoking, deep-fry the meatballs until they turn golden brown on the outside. Place them on paper towels to drain and cool.

Transfer the meatballs to a baking sheet and freeze, uncovered. When the meatballs are frozen, put them in an airtight container and return them to the freezer for up to 3 months.

LATER

Preheat the oven to 325°F. Transfer the frozen meatballs to a large roasting pan. Bake them for about 1 to 1½ hours until thoroughly heated, tossing the meatballs occasionally.

Combine the cornstarch and vinegar, mixing until the cornstarch has dissolved. Add the water, mix well, and set aside.

In a medium saucepan over medium-high heat combine the ginger, sugar, soy sauce, curry powder, and cornstarch mixture, stirring until the sauce has thickened. Remove from heat and stir in the pineapple chunks. Just before serving, pour the warm sauce over the meatballs and serve with toothpicks.

TIP One secret to this recipe is not to put the meatballs in the sauce until you're ready to serve. If they're put in the sauce too early, they become soggy and often fall apart.

Makes about 60 meatballs

Mexican Layered Dip

*We should call this "Señor Houdini Dip" because of the way it simply
disappears after your guests arrive.*

NOW
2 cups sour cream
1 package (1¼ ounces) taco seasoning
One 9-ounce can bean dip
1 cup guacamole
6 to 8 green onions (scallions), finely chopped
One 4¼ ounce can chopped ripe olives
1 cup salsa
2 medium tomatoes, finely chopped and drained
2 cups shredded cheddar-Jack cheese (or use cheddar or Monterey Jack
    cheese, or a combination)

LATER
Corn chips, for serving

NOW

Combine the sour cream and taco seasoning mix in a small bowl, and set
aside.

Spread the bean dip over the bottom of a 9-inch pie dish. Top with the
guacamole, carefully spreading it to completely cover the bean dip. Top
with a layer of the green onions followed by the olives, salsa, and tomatoes.
Top with a layer of the sour cream mixture, spreading it to the edges of the

dish to seal. Sprinkle the cheese over the top. Cover tightly and refrigerate for 2 hours or overnight.

LATER

Unwrap the dip, and serve it with corn chips.

Serves 6 to 8

"What's in This?" Pico de Gallo

Your guests will love the heady aroma of freshly roasted cumin seeds in this salsa—a startlingly delicious secret ingredient.

NOW

4 teaspoons cumin seeds

1 large garlic clove, minced

1 tablespoon lemon juice, plus more if needed

1 teaspoon minced jalapeño pepper (omit if you don't like heat)

2 green onions (scallions), chopped

$1/3$ cup minced onion

$1/2$ teaspoon salt

$1/4$ teaspoon freshly ground black pepper

3 tablespoons finely chopped cilantro, plus more if desired

1 medium-sized ripe Haas avocado, diced

$1/2$ pint cherry tomatoes, quartered

LATER

Tortilla chips, for serving

NOW

Toast the cumin seeds by putting them in a dry skillet on high for about 2 minutes, shaking the pan frequently, until they start popping. Transfer the toasted seeds to a cutting board and, using a large, flat-bladed knife, chop them up very finely.

In a medium serving bowl, combine the garlic, lemon juice, jalapeño, green onions, onion, salt, pepper, cilantro, and avocado. Mix carefully, trying not to mash the avocado too much. Add the cherry tomatoes last and mix gently.

If you plan to serve the dip within 2 to 3 hours, leave it at room temperature, covered with plastic wrap until needed. If you plan to serve it later, sprinkle an additional teaspoon of lemon juice over the top to help prevent the avocado from turning brownish. Cover with plastic wrap and refrigerate overnight or up to 24 hours.

LATER

Serve with tortilla chips. Sprinkle an additional teaspoon of chopped cilantro on top if you want.

Serves 4

Olive Cheese Puffs

These puffs are tasty pimiento-stuffed olives surrounded by a light, airy cheese crust. The best part about these appetizers is that they can be kept in the freezer, ready to go for sudden guests or an instant party.

48 pimiento stuffed olives, drained
2 cups grated sharp cheddar cheese, at room temperature
$1/2$ cup butter (1 stick), softened
1 cup flour
$1/2$ teaspoon salt
1 teaspoon paprika

NOW

Put the drained olives on paper towels to dry thoroughly. Combine the cheese with the butter and beat vigorously with an electric beater until smooth. Add the flour, salt, and paprika, and mix until smooth. Wrap I teaspoon of the pastry dough around each olive, covering it completely. Place them on a baking sheet and freeze, uncovered. When frozen, transfer the olives to an airtight container and return them to the freezer for up to 3 months

LATER

Preheat the oven to 400°F. Place the frozen olive balls on an ungreased baking sheet, and bake for 15 minutes, or until lightly browned.

Makes 48 puffs

Fresh Mushroom Pâté

A unique, creamy pâté with a rich flavor, best when made a day or two in advance. It just gets better and better.

NOW
2 tablespoons unsalted butter
2 tablespoons dry sherry
$^1/_2$ pound sliced fresh mushrooms, coarsely chopped
One 4-ounce package garlic and herb cheese spread
$^1/_2$ cup cream cheese (4 ounces)

LATER
Crackers, for serving

NOW

Heat the butter and sherry in a medium skillet over medium heat. Add the mushrooms and sauté for 5 to 10 minutes, until the mushrooms are tender and almost all the liquid has evaporated. Transfer to a blender or food processor with the cheese spread and cream cheese, and process until creamy. Transfer the pâté to a cheese crock or serving dish, smoothing the top with a rubber spatula. Cover tightly and refrigerate for at least 3 hours or up to 3 days.

LATER

Remove the pâté from the refrigerator and allow it to soften to a spreadable consistency, about 1 hour. Serve with crackers.

TIP This pâté is best refrigerated in an airtight container. Do not store it in the freezer!

Serves 6 to 8

Minnetonka Turnovers

These turnovers are worth the effort and look just as good on a cheese tray as they look on a silver serving platter. In the beautiful lake country woods around Minnetonka, Minnesota, you can be as rustic or as elegant as you wish—and these turnovers would be in style. This recipe offers three options for fillings, so you can make one or all.

Pastry
1 cup cream cheese (8 ounces), softened
$1/2$ cup butter (1 stick), softened
$1^1/_2$ cups all-purpose flour

Filling Option 1: Mushroom
1 large onion, minced
3 tablespoons butter
$1/2$ pound fresh mushrooms, finely chopped
1 teaspoon dried thyme
$1/2$ teaspoon salt
Pepper
2 tablespoons all-purpose flour
$1/4$ cup sour cream

Filling Option 2: Ham
1 cup finely chopped cooked ham
1 cup cream cheese with chives (8 ounces), softened
$1/4$ cup sweet pickles, finely chopped and drained

Filling Option 3: Crab

1 cup fresh or canned crabmeat
$^1/_2$ cup mayonnaise
$^1/_2$ cup grated sharp cheddar or Swiss cheese
1 green onion (scallion), minced
1 teaspoon prepared horseradish, optional

NOW

Pastry

Using an electric beater, beat the cream cheese and butter together. Add the flour and blend until smooth. Pat the dough into a ball, cover, and refrigerate for 30 minutes. While the pastry is chilling, make one of the fillings:

Mushroom Filling

Lightly sauté the onions in butter over medium heat, just until they begin to soften. Add the mushrooms and cook for 5 minutes more until the mushrooms are soft and the onions are transparent. Add the thyme, salt, and pepper, and mix well. Sprinkle the flour on top and mix well. Stir in the sour cream and cook, stirring frequently, until the mixture has thickened, about 5 minutes. Set aside.

Ham Filling

Combine all the ingredients in a medium bowl. Set aside.

Crab Filling

Combine all the ingredients in a medium bowl. Set aside

When your filling of choice is ready, cut the pastry ball in half and roll the dough out to a $^1/_8$-inch thickness on a lightly floured board. Cut into 3-inch rounds. Place 1 teaspoon filling in the center of each round, and fold the dough over the filling. Press the edges closed with a fork, and prick small holes in the top of each turnover.

Place the turnovers on baking sheets, and freeze, uncovered. When they are thoroughly frozen, transfer to an airtight container, and return them to the freezer for up to 3 months.

LATER

Preheat the oven to 425°F. Place the frozen turnovers on an ungreased baking sheet, and bake for 15 to 20 minutes, until lightly browned.

Makes 48 turnovers

✳ Embassy Row Elegant Pâté

Even people who don't like liver will enjoy this very sophisticated pâté.

NOW
1¹/₂ pounds chicken livers
¹/₂ onion
2 teaspoons salt
1 dash of cayenne pepper
¹/₂ cup margarine (1 stick), no substitute
³/₄ teaspoon nutmeg
3 teaspoons dry mustard
¹/₄ teaspoon ground cloves
¹/₃ cup finely minced red onion

LATER
1 egg, hard-cooked, peeled and finely grated
Crackers or mini-bagels, for serving

NOW

Place the chicken livers in a medium saucepan and cover with water. Add the onion and salt. Cook over medium-high heat until the livers are tender and no longer pink in the middle, about 15 minutes. Drain, discarding the water and the onion.

Put the livers in a food processor, and add the cayenne, margarine, nutmeg, mustard, cloves, and red onion. Process until smooth. Transfer the pâté to a serving bowl and cover tightly with plastic wrap, or to an airtight container if you plan to freeze it. Refrigerate for up to 5 days, or freeze for up to 3 months.

LATER

If refrigerated, unwrap the pâté, garnish with the grated egg, and serve with crackers or mini-bagels. If frozen, transfer from the freezer to the refrigerator the night before you plan to use it. Before serving, mix thoroughly, transfer to a serving bowl, and garnish with the grated egg.

Makes 2 cups pâté

Montgomery Square Cocktail Pizzas

Montgomery Square is in Maryland, just outside of Washington, D.C. That's where we learned that these miniature pizzas are a hit with tots, teenagers, Washington Redskins fans—almost everyone! They're perfect for birthday parties, teen gatherings, cocktail parties, or family snacks.

1 pound sausage meat, cooked, crumbled, and drained

1 cup finely chopped onion

1 cup grated sharp cheddar cheese

1/2 cup grated Parmesan cheese

2 teaspoons dried oregano

1 teaspoon garlic salt

One 8-ounce can tomato sauce

One 6-ounce can tomato paste

Three 12-ounce cans refrigerated flaky biscuit dough

NOW

In a medium saucepan, combine the cooked sausage, onion, cheeses, oregano, garlic salt, tomato sauce, and tomato paste. Cook, stirring frequently, over medium heat, until the pizza sauce begins to bubble, about 15 minutes.

Separate each biscuit into 3 rounds, and place the rounds on baking sheets. Spread each round with the pizza sauce, and freeze, uncovered. When completely frozen, transfer the pizzas to an airtight container and return them to the freezer for up to 3 months.

LATER
Preheat the oven to 425°F. Lightly coat a baking sheet with vegetable oil spray. Place the pizzas on the prepared baking sheet, and bake for 10 minutes, until lightly browned. Serve immediately.

TIP Don't spend too much time trying to pull apart each biscuit into 3 equal pieces: it doesn't matter if they are different thicknesses.

Makes about 90 cocktail pizzas

Pepperoni Pizza Dip

Looks great, tastes great! If you don't have pita chips, use your favorite crackers.

NOW
2 cups cream cheese (16 ounces), softened
$1/2$ cup sour cream
1 teaspoon dried crumbled oregano
$1/4$ teaspoon garlic powder
$1/4$ teaspoon crushed red pepper flakes
1 cup finely chopped pepperoni
$1/4$ cup thinly sliced green onions (scallions)
$1/4$ cup finely chopped green bell pepper

LATER

1 cup prepared pizza sauce

1 to 2 cups shredded mozzarella cheese

Pita chips, for serving

NOW

Lightly grease a 9- or 10-inch quiche dish or pie pan, and set aside. In a medium bowl, beat together the cream cheese, sour cream, oregano, garlic powder, and red pepper flakes with an electric beater until well mixed. Add the pepperoni, green onion, and bell pepper, and mix well. Pour the cream cheese mixture into the prepared baking dish. Cover tightly and refrigerate for up to 3 days.

LATER

Preheat the oven to 350°F. Unwrap the dip and spread the pizza sauce over the top. Bake for 15 minutes. Top with the mozzarella cheese, and bake 10 minutes more, or until the cheese is melted. Serve with pita chips.

Serves 6 to 8

Ping-Pong Sausage Balls

It may not be possible to make enough of these, since they are so popular and easy to eat. Perfect for a cocktail party, they're also great served at a coffee klatch because they are a little more substantial than rolls.

1 pound sausage meat (hot or mild)
8 ounces cheddar cheese, shredded (about 2 cups)
3 cups biscuit mix
$\frac{1}{4}$ cup water

NOW

Combine all the ingredients until well-mixed. Form the sausage mixture into walnut-sized balls. Place the balls on baking sheets and freeze, uncovered. When the balls are frozen, transfer them to an airtight container and return them to the freezer for up to 3 months.

LATER

Preheat the oven to 350°F. Transfer the frozen balls to an ungreased baking sheet, and bake for 25 to 30 minutes, until browned. Serve warm.

Makes 50 to 60 balls

Spinach Balls

Popeye would love these!

Two 10-ounce packages frozen chopped spinach, thawed and squeezed dry
2 cups Pepperidge Farm herb seasoned stuffing mix, crushed
2 medium onions, finely chopped
4 eggs, lightly beaten
$^1/_2$ cup margarine (1 stick), melted
1 tablespoon garlic salt
$^1/_2$ teaspoon dried thyme
$^1/_2$ teaspoon pepper
$^1/_2$ cup grated Parmesan cheese

NOW

In a medium bowl, combine all the ingredients until well mixed. Roll the spinach mixture into walnut-sized balls. Place the balls on baking sheets and freeze, uncovered. Once the balls are frozen, transfer them to an airtight container and return them to the freezer for up to 3 months.

LATER

Preheat the oven to 350°F. Arrange the frozen balls on a lightly greased baking sheet, and bake for 20 minutes until lightly browned. Serve immediately.

TIP   This is another great make-ahead dish to always have in the freezer, ready for surprise guests or hungry kids arriving home from school.

Makes about 72 balls

Heritage Spinach Dip

Always a favorite! This dip is best if you make it at least one day ahead, to blend the flavors.

NOW

One 10-ounce package frozen chopped spinach, thawed and squeezed dry

2 cups sour cream

1 cup mayonnaise

1 package (1.4 ounces) Knorr vegetable soup mix

1 package (0.7 ounce) Good Seasons Italian salad dressing mix

One 5-ounce can water chestnuts, drained and finely chopped

$1/4$ cup finely chopped red onion

1 tablespoon Worcestershire sauce

LATER

Cocktail bread, crackers, pita chips, or fresh vegetables, for dipping

NOW

In a medium bowl, stir together the spinach, sour cream, mayonnaise, soup mix, salad dressing mix, water chestnuts, onions, and Worcestershire sauce. Cover and refrigerate for 2 hours up to 2 days.

LATER

Unwrap the dip and serve with cocktail bread, crackers, pita chips, or fresh vegetables.

Makes about 4 cups dip

Salsa Linda

The title means "beautiful sauce" in Spanish, and it's so good you can eat it by the spoonful.

NOW

Two 4¼-ounce cans chopped ripe olives

One 4-ounce can diced green chiles

4 to 6 green onions (scallions), chopped

2 medium tomatoes, finely diced

3 tablespoons olive oil

2 tablespoons red wine vinegar

1 teaspoon garlic salt

1 tablespoon hot salsa or hot pepper sauce, optional

LATER

Tortilla chips, for serving

NOW

Combine all the ingredients in a medium bowl and mix well. Refrigerate, covered, for up to 5 days.

LATER

Drain and save most of the liquid. Put the salsa in a serving bowl, and serve with tortilla chips. If you have leftovers, store with the liquid in an airtight container.

TIP This salsa is great on top of nachos, quesadillas, or other Mexican fare.

Makes 2 cups salsa

Soups and Salads

In our house we give top priority to hearty soups and fresh, inventive salads. Our primary secret is to stay away from familiar, everyday fare. Tossed salads need a variety of colorful lettuces and other bright ingredients with contrasting textures, such as chunks of cheese, mandarin oranges, and large pieces of crystallized walnuts. Soups should feature tastes and aromas that will trigger the "good memory" section of your brain.

The term "make-ahead" is, of course, never far from our thoughts. Even a tossed salad can be prepared hours in advance—and a salad dressing is the quintessential make-ahead recipe. Like a stew, the flavors of a dressing improve greatly if you make it at least a day in advance. Since salads are the dish where contrasts are most expected in your menu, your salad ingredients should be a mixture of soft and crunchy, and your dressing should have a combination of tart and sweet flavors.

Plan to add your dressing at serving time, and then go ahead and place the salad fixings in your salad bowl and store it in the refrigerator. The secret is to layer the ingredients, placing wet items like tomatoes and chopped vegetables on the bottom and drier items such as lettuce and cheeses on top. Cover with a damp paper towel, refrigerate, and the salad will keep in this way all day. You can toss it with the dressing at the last minute, just before serving.

Salad dressings and soups release wonderful tastes when you refrigerate them overnight or even longer. They seem to cry out for you to make them ahead of time, so get started with these recipes! We bet that you'll serve many of these delicious soups and salads as your main course from time to time.

Zucchini Paradise Soup

A touch of curry gives a zing to this tasty soup, which works well hot or cold.

NOW

2 tablespoons butter

2 tablespoons finely chopped onion

1 large clove garlic, minced

1 pound zucchini, thinly sliced (about 2^1/$_2$ cups)

^{1}/$_4$ teaspoon curry powder (use 1 teaspoon if you plan to serve the soup cold)

^{1}/$_2$ teaspoon salt

^{1}/$_2$ cup evaporated milk

1^1/$_4$ cups chicken broth

LATER

Freshly chopped parsley, for garnish

NOW

Place the butter, onion, garlic, and zucchini in a large skillet with a tightly fitting lid. Cook, covered, over medium heat for about 10 minutes, shaking the pan frequently to prevent sticking. Transfer the vegetables to a blender. Add the curry powder, salt, evaporated milk, and broth, and blend for 30 seconds, until pureed. Allow the mixture to cool, and transfer to an airtight container. Refrigerate overnight or up to 4 days, or freeze for up to 3 months.

LATER

If frozen, allow the soup to thaw in the refrigerator overnight. If it is to be served cold, stir and serve. If it is to be served warm, heat it in a medium pot over low heat, stirring occasionally. Top each serving with a sprinkling of parsley.

Serves 4

Beans! Beans! Bean Soup

The legions of people who love bean dishes will line up for this soup.

One 15-ounce can pinto beans
One 4-ounce can diced green chiles
Two 15-ounce cans navy (white) beans
Two 16-ounce cans bean and bacon soup
1 large onion, finely chopped
1 cup finely chopped ham
1 cup water

NOW

Preheat the oven to 300°F, or set out a crock pot. Combine all the ingredients in a large bowl, mixing well. Transfer to a large covered casserole or to a crock pot. Bake for 2 hours, or cook in a crockpot on high heat for 4 hours. Allow the mixture to cool, and transfer it to an airtight container. Refrigerate overnight or up to 4 days, or freeze for up to 3 months.

LATER

If frozen, allow the soup to thaw in the refrigerator overnight. Reheat in a large pot over medium heat. stirring occasionally, until the soup is thoroughly warmed.

TIP If you would like your soup spicier, substitute one 15-ounce can of pinto beans with jalapeños. Omit the can of green chiles.

Serves 6

Lentil Soup

A nutritious soup that's also delicious.

NOW

3 tablespoons butter
3 stalks celery, finely chopped
2 medium carrots, finely chopped
1 medium leek (white part only), finely chopped
1 medium onion, finely chopped
3 tablespoons flour
6 cups hot chicken broth
1 bay leaf
$^1/_2$ teaspoon dried thyme
$1^1/_2$ cups dried lentils
2 teaspoons salt
$^1/_2$ teaspoon pepper

LATER

Croutons, for serving

NOW

In a large pot, melt the butter over medium heat. Add the celery, carrot, leek, and onion. Cook, stirring frequently, until the vegetables are tender and lightly browned, about 10 minutes. Stir in the flour, and cook the vegetables for 2 minutes more. Remove from heat. Slowly stir in 1 cup of the broth, mixing and stirring until smooth.

Over high heat, add the remaining 5 cups broth, and bring to a boil. Stir in the bay leaf, thyme, lentils, and salt and pepper, and reduce heat to low. Cover loosely, and simmer for $1^1/_4$ to $1^1/_2$ hours, until the lentils are very tender. Remove from heat, and remove and discard the bay leaf. Puree the soup using an immersion blender, or in batches in an upright blender. Adjust salt and pepper to taste. Cool, cover, and refrigerate overnight or up to 4 days.

LATER
Slowly reheat the soup over medium-low heat. Top each serving with several croutons.

TIP For a heartier soup, you can add precooked, diced kielbasa (Polish sausage).

Serves 6

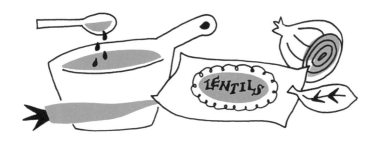

Pioneer Vegetable Soup

This hearty soup is great comfort food.

NOW

2 pounds beef stew meat, cut into small pieces

6 cups water

One 28-ounce can crushed tomatoes (3¼ cups)

½ cup red wine

4 to 6 beef bouillon cubes

1 tablespoon salt

2 teaspoons pepper

1 teaspoon sugar

1 large onion, finely chopped

1 tablespoon Worcestershire sauce

4 large celery ribs, thinly sliced

4 medium carrots, thinly sliced

One 10-ounce package frozen green beans

One 10-ounce package frozen corn

LATER

3 medium potatoes, peeled and cut into small cubes

NOW

In a large pot, combine the beef, water, tomatoes, wine, bouillon cubes, salt, pepper, sugar, onion, and Worcestershire sauce. Bring to a boil over high heat. Reduce the heat to low and simmer, stirring occasionally, for 1 to 2 hours, until the beef is tender. Remove from heat and stir in the celery, carrots, green beans, and corn. Let the soup cool. Transfer it to an airtight container, and freeze for up to 3 months.

Transfer the frozen soup to the refrigerator, and allow it to thaw overnight. Pour the soup into a large pot. Bring it to a simmer over medium heat, and reduce the heat to low. Add the potatoes and continue simmering just until they become tender, about 20 minutes.

TIP Here are some easy substitutions:
  ✧ Use 1 cup small elbow macaroni instead of the potato cubes.
  ✧ Use a 1-pound package of frozen mixed vegetables instead of the carrots, green beans, and corn.

Serves 12

Gazpacho

This is so pretty and just perfect on a warm, sunny day.

NOW
8 large tomatoes, peeled
2 medium green bell peppers
8 green onions (scallions)
1 red onion
2 large cucumbers, peeled and seeds removed
Salt and pepper

LATER

5 large cloves garlic, crushed

¹/₂ cup vegetable oil

1 tablespoon seasoned salt

¹/₃ cup red wine vinegar

1 teaspoon white pepper

1 tablespoon ground cumin

4 cups vegetable juice cocktail or tomato juice

2 cups water

NOW

Very finely chop the tomatoes, bell peppers, green onions, red onion, and cucumbers. Transfer to a large bowl, and season the vegetables with salt and pepper to taste. Cover and refrigerate for up to 24 hours.

LATER

In another large bowl, combine the garlic, vegetable oil, seasoned salt, vinegar, white pepper, and cumin, and mix well. Add the chilled vegetable mixture, and any accumulated juices, and mix well. Stir in the vegetable juice and water. Refrigerate for 4 to 8 hours, and mix well before serving.

TIP For a spicier gazpacho, substitute 2 cups Bloody Mary mix and 2 cups vegetable juice cocktail or tomato juice for the 4 cups vegetable juice cocktail or tomato juice.

Serves 8 to 10

Pumpkin Soup with Sage Croutons

This soup highlights the deep, rich flavors of autumn.

NOW

2 tablespoons unsalted butter
1 large carrot, finely chopped
1 large onion, finely chopped
2 stalks celery, finely chopped
$1/2$ bay leaf
$1/4$ teaspoon dried sage, crumbled
Salt and pepper
One 16-ounce can pumpkin puree
4 cups chicken broth

LATER

1 cup chicken broth
Salt and pepper
2 slices white bread, crusts removed and lightly buttered
1 teaspoon dried sage, crumbled
8 small fresh sage leaves

NOW

Melt the butter in a large pot over medium heat. Add the carrot, onion, celery, bay leaf, and sage. Season with salt and pepper to taste. Cook, stirring occasionally, until the vegetables have softened, about 10 minutes. Stir in the pureed pumpkin, and add the broth, 1 cup at a time. Increase the heat to medium-high and bring to a boil. Reduce the heat to low, and simmer, stirring occasionally, for 15 minutes more.

Remove and discard the bay leaf. Puree the soup using an immersion blender, or puree it in batches in an upright blender or food processor. Allow the soup to cool. Transfer to an airtight container, and refrigerate for up to 3 days.

LATER

Return the soup to a large pot, and bring it to a boil on medium-high heat. Stir in enough of the broth to obtain your desired consistency. Season with salt and pepper to taste.

Preheat the oven to 350°F. While the soup is heating, cut both slices of bread into 4 squares, and halve them on a diagonal to form triangles. Place the triangles on a baking sheet, and sprinkle them with the dried sage. Bake until golden brown, about 15 minutes. Top each serving of the soup with the sage croutons and a fresh sage leaf.

Serves 8

Mah-velous Minestrone!

This soup has everything in it, so it will hit the spot for everybody.

> 2 tablespoons vegetable oil
> 2 pounds beef stew meat, cut into $^1/_2$-inch cubes
> 2$^1/_2$ quarts water
> 3 large carrots, thinly sliced
> 2 small turnips (about $^1/_2$ pound total), cut into $^1/_8$-inch-thick strips
> 1 small head cabbage, shredded

1 large onion, finely chopped

4 beef bouillon cubes

One 28-ounce can crushed tomatoes

$^1/_2$ cup barley

2 teaspoons salt

1 bay leaf

One 15-ounce can kidney beans, undrained

$^1/_2$ cup finely chopped parsley

6 ounces spaghetti, broken into 2-inch pieces

$^1/_2$ cup freshly grated Parmesan cheese

NOW

In a large pot or Dutch oven, heat the oil over medium-high heat. Add the beef and cook, stirring frequently, until the beef has browned, 5 to 7 minutes. Stir in the water, carrots, turnips, cabbage, onion, bouillon cubes, tomatoes, barley, salt, and bay leaf, and bring to a boil. Reduce the heat to low, cover, and simmer for at least 1 hour, until the vegetables are tender. Remove and discard the bay leaf. Stir in the beans and their liquid, parsley, spaghetti, and cheese.

Remove the soup from heat, and allow it to cool for about 1 hour. Cover and refrigerate overnight. If freezing, transfer the soup to an airtight container, and freeze for up to 3 months. If not, the soup can remain in the refrigerator up to 3 more days.

LATER

If frozen, allow the soup to thaw overnight in the refrigerator. Transfer the soup to a large pot, and slowly reheat it over low heat until thoroughly warmed.

Serves 12 to 14

Durango Corn Chowder

Cowboys stirring the campfire pot under darkening Southwestern skies would sure have liked this one! We think this soup is best made one day ahead.

NOW
3 tablespoons butter or margarine
1 large onion, finely chopped
1 medium green bell pepper, finely chopped
1 clove garlic, minced
One 4-ounce can chopped green chiles
One 15-ounce can diced tomatoes, drained and broken into small pieces
Two 15-ounce cans creamed corn
One 15-ounce can corn
2 cups chicken broth, plus more if needed
1 cup milk
2 cups finely chopped cooked chicken
1 tablespoon hot taco sauce, optional

LATER
4 ounces Monterey Jack cheese, shredded (1 cup)
$^1/_2$ cup finely chopped cilantro
1 cup crushed tortilla chips

NOW

Melt the butter in a large pot over medium heat. Add the onion, bell pepper, and garlic. Cook, stirring frequently, until the onion is tender, about 5 minutes. Add the chiles and tomatoes and mix well. Stir in the creamed corn and regular corn, the broth, milk, chicken, and taco sauce if using. Increase the heat to medium-high and bring to a boil. Reduce the heat to low and simmer the soup for 30 minutes more. Remove the soup from heat and allow it to cool. Transfer to an airtight container, and refrigerate overnight or for up to 3 days.

LATER

Pour the soup into a large pot and add more broth if it needs thinning. Stir in the cheese and heat the soup over low heat, stirring frequently, until the cheese has melted. Top each serving with a sprinkling of cilantro and crushed chips.

Serves 6

✳ Party Salad for Ten

One of Mother's best recipes. It's enormously popular as the centerpiece of a fine luncheon.

NOW

1 cup sour cream

2 cups mayonnaise

8 to 10 ounces fresh spinach (1 bunch), cleaned and torn into pieces

Salt and pepper

1 teaspoon sugar, divided

6 hard-boiled eggs, peeled and finely chopped

$^1/_2$ large head iceberg lettuce, shredded

$^1/_2$ pound sliced boiled ham, cut into thin strips

10 ounces frozen peas, thawed and drained

1 large red onion, thinly sliced into rings

$^1/_2$ pound sliced Swiss cheese, cut into thin strips

LATER

$1/2$ pound bacon, cooked crisp and crumbled, or 2.8 ounces bacon bits

NOW

Combine the sour cream and mayonnaise in a small bowl, mixing well. Set aside.

In a large serving bowl, layer the salad: First, lay a bed of the spinach. Season with salt and pepper to taste, and sprinkle with $1/2$ teaspoon of the sugar. Spread the eggs evenly over the spinach. Spread the lettuce over the eggs. Season again with salt and pepper to taste, and sprinkle with the remaining $1/2$ teaspoon sugar. Follow with the ham, the peas, and then the onion rings. Spread the mayonnaise dressing over the top of the salad, making sure to coat it from edge to edge. Top with the cheese strips. Cover tightly and refrigerate overnight.

LATER

Uncover the salad, and top it with the crumbled bacon. (Do not toss!) Be sure to scoop all the way to the bottom of the bowl when serving each portion.

TIP You can substitute cooked crabmeat or shrimp for the bacon.

Serves 10 to 15

Blue Cheese–Grape Salad

This colorful salad makes a wonderful presentation: the blue cheese, grapes, and raspberry vinegar are a study in contrasting flavors and textures.

NOW

$1/4$ cup raspberry vinegar

1 tablespoon Dijon mustard

1 tablespoon sugar

1 teaspoon salt

$1/2$ teaspoon pepper

$2/3$ cup olive oil

LATER

2 ounces crumbled blue cheese ($1/2$ cup)

7 cups mixed leaf lettuce, cleaned and torn into bite-sized pieces

1 cup seedless grapes, halved

$1/2$ medium red onion, thinly sliced

2 cups radicchio, torn into bite-sized pieces, optional

1 cup croutons, optional

NOW

Combine the vinegar, mustard, sugar, salt, and pepper in a blender. Mix well on low speed, then very slowly add the oil until it is all incorporated. Transfer to an airtight container, and refrigerate for up to 2 weeks.

LATER

Shake the dressing until thoroughly combined. In a large bowl, combine the blue cheese, lettuce, grapes, onion, and the radicchio if desired. Toss with the dressing until well combined. Top with the croutons if desired.

TIP   In tossed salads, try to use 3 different kinds of lettuce for variety. Also, any salad will be mixed thoroughly if you toss it exactly 13 times.

Serves 6 to 8

Mexican Cobb Salad

The taste and texture combinations are hard to beat in this Mexican take on the classic Cobb.

NOW
Dressing
1 cup sour cream
One 4-ounce can diced green chiles
$1/4$ cup coarsely chopped cilantro
2 tablespoons lime juice
$1/2$ teaspoon pepper
$1/4$ teaspoon salt
1 teaspoon ground cumin
Hot pepper sauce, optional

Salad

6 cups romaine lettuce, cleaned and torn into bite-sized pieces

One 15-ounce can kidney beans or black beans, drained

2 large tomatoes, diced

1½ cups chopped celery

2 cups cooked diced chicken

2 cups shredded cheddar-jack cheese (or use cheddar or Monterey Jack
cheese, or a combination of the two), divided

¼ cup finely chopped red onion

6 slices bacon, cooked and crumbled

LATER

1 avocado, coarsely chopped

1 cup salsa

NOW

To make the dressing, combine all the ingredients in a small bowl and mix well. Set aside. In a large bowl, layer the salad: First, lay a bed of the lettuce. Spread the beans evenly over the lettuce. Spread the tomatoes over the beans. Follow with the celery, the chicken, 1 cup of the cheese, the onion, and then the bacon. Spread the dressing over the top of the salad, from edge to edge. Top with the remaining 1 cup cheese. Cover tightly and refrigerate overnight or up to 3 days.

LATER

Uncover the salad and top with the avocado. Serve with the salsa on the side.

TIP This salad looks divine when layered in a clear glass bowl. Just make sure to take each layer to the edges so you can see the colors stack up.

Serves 4 to 6

Austin Pepper-Steak Salad

This refreshing main-course salad recipe comes with a "two-pack" of dressing choices.

NOW

Dressing Option 1: Green Peppercorn Vinaigrette

2 cups salad oil

$1/2$ teaspoon salt

3 dashes of hot pepper sauce

1 tablespoon lemon juice

$1/2$ teaspoon pepper

1 teaspoon Worcestershire sauce

$1/4$ cup red wine vinegar

2 tablespoons whole green peppercorns

Dressing Option 2: Teriyaki-Style Vinaigrette

$1^1/2$ cups teriyaki sauce

$1/3$ cup salad oil

$1/3$ cup dry sherry

3 tablespoons white vinegar

$1/2$ teaspoon ground ginger

Salad

3 cups thin strips of rare roast beef

1 pint cherry tomatoes

1 green bell pepper, thinly sliced

1 cup sliced celery

$1/3$ cup sliced green onions (scallions)

$1/2$ cup fresh mushrooms, sliced

LATER

LATER

4 cups mixed greens (such as Bibb, leaf, or romaine lettuce and savoy cabbage), cleaned and torn into bite-sized pieces

NOW

Choose one of the dressing options. Combine all the ingredients in a small bowl, and beat vigorously. Set aside.

To make the salad, combine the beef, tomatoes, bell pepper, celery, green onions, and mushrooms in a large bowl. Add the dressing to the beef mixture, and toss well to coat. Cover and refrigerate for 2 hours or up to 2 days.

LATER

Drain the beef mixture, reserving the liquid. Place the mixed greens in a large salad bowl. Top with the beef mixture and toss well. Serve the reserved liquid on the side, as a dressing.

Serves 4 to 6

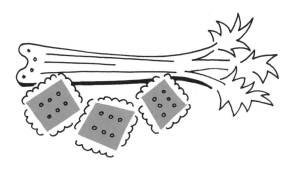

Mandarin Orange Salad

This salad goes well with any meal—and your guests will want the recipe before they leave! It is the most versatile salad we serve. If you're serving it with chicken or seafood, use rice vinegar for a mild flavor; if you're serving it with beef or veal, choose red wine vinegar for a stronger flavor.

NOW

⅓ cup sugar

1 teaspoon dry mustard

1 teaspoon celery seed

1 teaspoon salt

1 tablespoon dried minced onion

¼ cup rice or red wine vinegar

1 cup vegetable oil

LATER

1 large head Boston lettuce, cleaned and torn into bite-sized pieces

1 large head romaine lettuce, cleaned and torn into bite-sized pieces

1 cup salted peanuts

One 15-ounce can mandarin oranges, drained

NOW

Combine the sugar, mustard, celery seed, salt, onion, and vinegar in a blender. Mix well on low speed, then very slowly add the oil until it is all incorporated. (The dressing will be very thick.) Transfer to an airtight container, and refrigerate overnight or for up to 2 weeks.

LATER

In a large salad bowl, combine the Boston and romaine lettuce, peanuts, and orange slices. Beat the dressing to make sure it's emulsified, then add it to the salad and toss well.

Serves 8 to 10

Chinese Chicken Salad

This is one of our recipes that we make most often. It's crunchy, tasty, and easily doubled (or tripled). It is always a crowd-pleaser, so be sure to make enough.

NOW

Chicken

2 whole chicken breasts

3 slices fresh ginger, each about the size of a quarter

Dressing

$1/4$ cup sugar

1 teaspoon salt

1 teaspoon seasoned salt

$1/2$ teaspoon black pepper

$1/4$ cup rice vinegar

$1/2$ cup salad oil

Salad

3$^1/_2$ to 4 ounces Chinese rice sticks

Vegetable oil for deep-frying

$^1/_2$ cup slivered almonds

$^1/_2$ cup sesame seeds

LATER

Salad

1 head iceberg lettuce, finely shredded

6 green onions (scallions), sliced on a diagonal

1 medium red bell pepper, cored and cut into thin strips

8 ounces snow peas or snap peas

NOW

Place the chicken breasts in a medium saucepan. Add the ginger and enough water to cover the chicken. Bring to a boil. Cover, reduce the heat to a simmer, and cook for about 30 minutes, until the chicken is cooked through. Remove from heat, and allow the chicken to rest in the liquid, just until cool enough to handle.

Remove the chicken from the pan, reserving the liquid and the ginger slices. Shred the chicken into bite-sized morsels, and put the shredded chicken in an airtight container. Add the ginger slices, and cover with the reserved liquid. Refrigerate overnight or up to 3 days.

To make the dressing, combine the sugar, salt, seasoned salt, pepper, and vinegar in a medium saucepan. Cook over low heat for 10 minutes, stirring until all the solids are dissolved. (Do not allow to boil.) Let the mixture cool, 15 to 20 minutes, then whisk in the salad oil. Transfer to an airtight container and refrigerate. The dressing will keep for several weeks.

To make the salad, deep-fry the Chinese rice sticks according to package directions. Store in an airtight container for up to 3 days. Carefully toast the almonds and sesame seeds in a dry skillet over medium heat, stirring frequently, just until they begin to brown, about 2 minutes. Allow the almonds and sesame seeds to cool, and then store them in an airtight container for up to 3 days.

LATER

To finish the salad, put the lettuce, onions, bell pepper, and snow peas in a large serving bowl. Add the toasted almonds and sesame seeds. Drain the chicken (remove and discard the ginger slices) and add it to the salad. Stir the dressing and pour it over the salad. Toss well to thoroughly combine. Immediately before serving, add the fried rice sticks and toss again.

TIP   You can use canned chow mein noodles in place of the rice sticks.

Serves 4 to 6

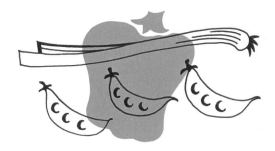

Piña Colada Chicken Salad

Our wonderful friend Katy always claimed she couldn't cook. Her children agreed, insisting that they never needed an alarm clock because Katy woke them up with the smoke alarm when she cooked breakfast! But with this wonderful recipe, which Katy made for us at her home one day, she proves that as a cook she has "the right stuff."

NOW
1 cup mayonnaise
1 cup piña colada or pineapple yogurt
1 teaspoon curry powder
4 cups cooked, diced chicken
1 cup whole seedless grapes
1 cup finely chopped celery
$1/2$ cup lightly toasted almond slivers (toss them in a dry skillet over high heat)
$1/2$ cup green onions (scallions), thinly sliced
One 8-ounce can crushed pineapple, well drained

LATER
6 to 8 large lettuce leaves

NOW

Combine the mayonnaise, yogurt, and curry powder in a small bowl. Mix well, and set aside. In a large bowl, combine the chicken, grapes, celery, almonds, onions, and pineapple. Add the yogurt dressing and toss to mix well. Cover tightly and refrigerate for several hours or up to 1 week.

LATER

Serve the chilled salad on a bed of lettuce.

Serves 4 to 6

Classic Spinach Salad

A tasty salad for luncheons or dinner.

NOW
Dressing
$1/4$ cup olive oil
$1/4$ teaspoon garlic salt
$1/3$ cup lemon juice
$1/2$ teaspoon salt
1 teaspoon Worcestershire sauce
$1/2$ cup grated Parmesan cheese
1 egg, lightly beaten *(see the Note on page 86 about the use of raw eggs)*

LATER

Salad

8 to 10 ounces fresh spinach (1 bunch), cleaned and torn into bite-sized
    pieces

1 medium red onion, sliced into thin rings

$1/4$ pound fresh mushrooms, sliced

1 large avocado, sliced lengthwise (sprinkle with 1 teaspoon lemon juice)

2 hard-cooked eggs, coarsely chopped

$1/2$ cup lightly toasted slivered almonds (toss them in a skillet over high heat)

Freshly ground black pepper

NOW

To make the dressing, combine the oil, garlic salt, lemon juice, salt, Worcestershire, Parmesan, and egg in a small bowl until well mixed. Transfer to an airtight container, and refrigerate for up to 3 days.

LATER

To make the salad, combine the spinach, onion, and mushrooms in a large bowl, tossing gently to mix. Transfer to an airtight container, or cover tightly with plastic wrap, and refrigerate for 2 to 8 hours.

Remove the dressing and the spinach mixture from the refrigerator. Shake the dressing until thoroughly combined. Toss salad with the dressing in a large serving bowl, and top with the avocado slices, eggs, and toasted almonds. Season with pepper to taste.

Serves 4 to 6

NOTE: *Although less than one percent of eggs have been found to harbor salmonella, all raw animal foods pose the risk of salmonella food poisoning. The stakes are higher for people who are pregnant, elderly, very young, or with compromised immune systems. These individuals should avoid raw and undercooked animal foods.*

To further minimize your risk of infection, you can either use pasteurized eggs (especially if there is no liquid in the recipe), or you can lightly beat the egg or eggs to be used with $^1/_4$ cup of liquid (per egg) from the recipe. Cook this mixture in a heavy saucepan over very low heat, stirring constantly, until the mixture coats a metal spoon, bubbles at the edges, or reaches 160°F. Cool quickly, and proceed with the recipe.

Main Line Dill Salad

This salad has made Scott famous—in our neighborhood, at least! Serve it and you're sure to get requests for the recipe. You can substitute blue cheese for the feta.

NOW

$^1/_4$ cup red wine vinegar

$^1/_2$ cup vegetable oil

3 tablespoons dried dill weed

1 tablespoon garlic salt

LATER

1 small head romaine lettuce, cleaned and cut into bite-sized pieces

1 small head iceberg lettuce, cleaned and cut into bite-sized pieces

1 small head Boston lettuce, cleaned and cut into bite-sized pieces

1 pint cherry tomatoes, halved

4 ounces feta cheese, crumbled (1 cup)

1 cucumber, thinly sliced

1 cup croutons, optional

In a small bowl, whisk together the vinegar, oil, dill, and garlic salt. Transfer to an airtight container, and refrigerate for up to 2 weeks.

LATER

In a large serving bowl, combine the lettuces, tomatoes, feta, and cucumber. Toss with the dressing, and top with the croutons if desired.

Serves 8 to 10

Spinach Salad with Poppy Seed Vinaigrette

Marinating a key ingredient—red onion—in the salad dressing overnight makes all the difference.

NOW

1 medium red onion, thinly sliced

$1^1/_2$ teaspoons poppy seeds

$^3/_4$ cup distilled white vinegar

$1^1/_2$ cups salad oil

$^1/_3$ cup sugar

1 tablespoon grated onion

$1^1/_2$ teaspoons salt

1 teaspoon dry mustard

8 to 10 ounces fresh spinach (1 bunch), cleaned and torn into bite-sized
pieces
1 small head iceberg lettuce, cleaned and torn into bite-sized pieces
$^1/_2$ pound Swiss cheese, grated (2 cups)
1 cup cottage cheese
$^1/_2$ pound bacon, cooked crisp and crumbled

NOW

Put the onion slices in an airtight container, and set aside.

Combine the poppy seeds, vinegar, oil, sugar, grated onion, salt, and
mustard in a blender. Mix well on low speed. Pour the dressing over the
onions. Cover and refrigerate overnight or up to 2 days.

LATER

In a large serving bowl, combine the spinach, lettuce, Swiss cheese, cottage
cheese, and bacon. Add the onion mixture and toss.

Serves 6 to 8

Romano Romaine Salad

Garlic oil is the secret ingredient here; it gives the dressing a sharp, rich taste.

NOW
4 cloves garlic
1 cup salad oil

LATER
1 egg, lightly beaten *(see the Note on page 86 about the use of raw eggs)*
Juice of 3 lemons
1 tablespoon Worcestershire sauce
1 tablespoon salt
1 tablespoon freshly ground black pepper
2 large heads well-chilled, crisp romaine lettuce, cleaned and cut into
    bite-sized pieces
$^1/_2$ cup freshly grated Romano cheese
1 cup croutons

NOW
Gently smash the garlic cloves with a heavy knife. Put the garlic in a jar with the oil, and shake well. Let it sit in a cool place for at least 1 week or up to 3 months.

LATER
Strain the garlic oil, discarding the garlic.

In a large bowl, combine the egg and lemon juice, and mix well. Add the garlic oil, Worcestershire sauce, salt, and pepper, and mix well. Add the lettuce, and toss until well combined. Top with the grated cheese and croutons.

Serves 6 to 8

Spinach Salad Extraordinaire

This is so much more than the common spinach salad. The Worcestershire sauce, avocados, Parmesan, and almond slivers combine to make this a tasty—and hearty—meal.

NOW

¹/₄ cup olive oil

¹/₄ teaspoon garlic salt

2 tablespoons red wine vinegar, or ¹/₃ cup lemon juice

¹/₂ teaspoon salt

1 teaspoon Worcestershire sauce

¹/₂ cup freshly grated Parmesan cheese

1 egg, lightly beaten *(see the Note on page 86 about the use of raw eggs)*

LATER

16 to 20 ounces fresh spinach (2 bunches), cleaned and torn into bite-sized pieces

¹/₄ pound fresh mushrooms

1 medium red onion

1 large or 2 small avocados

1 tablespoon lemon juice

2 hard-cooked eggs, sliced

¹/₂ cup lightly toasted almond slivers, optional (toss in a dry skillet over high heat)

1 cup croutons, optional

Freshly ground black pepper

NOW

In a small bowl, combine the oil, garlic salt, vinegar, salt, Worcestershire sauce, cheese, and egg, and mix well. Transfer to an airtight container, and refrigerate overnight or up to 3 days.

LATER

Toss the spinach, mushrooms, and onion in a large serving bowl. Cover and refrigerate for 2 to 6 hours.

Remove the spinach mixture and dressing from the refrigerator. Slice the avocado lengthwise and drizzle with the lemon juice. Toss the dressing with the spinach mixture, and mix well. Top with the avocado, eggs, toasted almonds, and croutons. Season with pepper to taste.

Serves 8 to 10

Tomato and Mozzarella Salad

Big, thick-sliced tomatoes, top-quality mozzarella, and fresh basil leaves will make this a summer highlight.

NOW
6 large tomatoes, sliced
15 whole fresh basil leaves, divided
1 red onion, thinly sliced
8 ounces mozzarella cheese, grated (2 cups)
3 tablespoons olive oil

3 tablespoons red wine vinegar
1 clove garlic, minced
1 teaspoon dried oregano
Salt and pepper

LATER
Lettuce leaves, to cover platter

NOW
In a shallow bowl, layer the tomatoes, 12 of the basil leaves, onion, and mozzarella. Mince the remaining 3 basil leaves. In a small bowl, combine the minced basil, oil, vinegar, garlic, and oregano until well mixed. Season with salt and pepper to taste. Drizzle the dressing over the tomato and mozzarella mixture. Cover and refrigerate for 3 hours or up to 2 days.

LATER
Cover a serving platter with the lettuce leaves. Carefully transfer the tomato and mozzarella mixture to the platter, alternating slices of tomato, onion, and the basil leaves. Drizzle with the remaining liquid from the storage container.

TIP Leftovers are great on sandwiches.

Serves 8 to 10

Hong Kong Slaw

This crunchy, fabulous salad will have everyone wondering where you got the recipe (and asking if they can they get it, too).

NOW
$^3/_4$ cup vegetable oil
$^1/_4$ cup rice vinegar
2 tablespoons soy sauce
$^1/_3$ cup plus 2 tablespoons sugar, divided
$^1/_2$ cup butter (1 stick)
6 ounces ramen noodles (discard flavor packets), crushed
$^1/_2$ cup slivered almonds
$^1/_2$ cup sesame seeds

LATER
2 heads Napa (Chinese) cabbage or bok choy, thinly sliced
4 fresh green onions (scallions), sliced on a diagonal into 1-inch pieces

NOW
Combine the oil, vinegar, soy sauce, and $^1/_3$ cup of the sugar, stirring until the sugar is dissolved completely. Transfer to an airtight container, and refrigerate for up to 1 week.

Melt the butter in a large skillet on medium heat. Add the noodles, almonds, sesame seeds, and the remaining 2 tablespoons sugar. Increase the heat to medium-high, and cook, stirring frequently, until the noodle mixture is golden brown. Drain the contents of the skillet on paper towels, and allow the toasted noodle mixture to cool completely. Transfer to an airtight container, and keep in a cool place for up to 3 days.

LATER

In a large serving bowl, combine the cabbage and the green onions. Top with the noodle mixture. Remove the dressing from the refrigerator, and mix well. Drizzle over the salad and toss well.

TIP You can buy "Oriental Flavor" ramen noodles and add 1 flavor packet to the dressing. Also, this salad is great with leftover grilled chicken—just dice it and toss it in.

Serves 6 to 8

Green Bean Salad

This tasty side salad is so simple, and you won't believe how popular it is. It goes well with any barbecue menu.

NOW
Two 28-ounce cans cut green beans, finely chopped
$1/2$ cup brown sugar
1 small red onion, finely chopped

LATER
$1/2$ cup mayonnaise, or more if needed
$1/2$ pound bacon, cooked crisp and crumbled
Salt and pepper

NOW
Drain the cans of green beans, reserving about $1^1/2$ cups liquid. Combine the brown sugar and reserved bean liquid in a large bowl, mixing until well combined. Add the green beans and onion, and mix well. Cover and refrigerate for 4 hours or overnight.

LATER
Drain the green bean mixture well. In a large bowl, combine it with the mayonnaise and bacon, and mix well. (Add a little more mayonnaise, if necessary, to bind the ingredients together.) Season with salt and pepper to taste. Serve cold or at room temperature.

Serves 8 to 10

Chinese Chicken and Pasta Salad

The tangy, piquant dressing sets this easy salad apart from the rest.

Pasta
1 pound angel hair pasta
1 tablespoon vegetable oil
1 pound boneless, skinless chicken breasts, cut into thin strips
1 medium red bell pepper, cut into thin strips
$1/4$ pound snap peas or snow peas, cut in half

Dressing
$1/4$ cup red wine vinegar
3 tablespoon dark or roasted sesame oil
2 tablespoons Dijon mustard
2 teaspoons sugar
2 tablespoons soy sauce
2 cloves garlic, minced
1 teaspoon freshly grated ginger
1 pinch of white pepper
2 tablespoons toasted sesame seeds (toss in a dry skillet over high heat)
$1/2$ cup finely chopped fresh cilantro

NOW

Cook the pasta according to package directions and drain it. Put it in a large serving bowl and set aside to cool.

Heat the oil in a wok or skillet over high heat. Add the chicken, bell pepper, and peas, and stir-fry for 3 minutes or until the chicken is cooked through. Remove from heat, and combine the chicken mixture with the pasta. Set aside.

To make the dressing, combine all the ingredients in a large jar. Cover tightly and shake vigorously until thoroughly mixed. Toss with the pasta and chicken salad, and refrigerate, covered with plastic wrap, for at least 2 hours or up to 2 days.

LATER
Unwrap the salad and toss thoroughly.

Serves 4 to 6

Greek Isles Pasta Salad

Picture yourself on the white, sun-drenched porch of a Greek island villa, and you should practically be able to taste the cool flavors of this delightful salad.

Salad
1 pound rotini pasta (tricolor is pretty)
6 ounces feta cheese, crumbled (1^1/$_2$ cups)
1 pint cherry tomatoes, halved
1 cucumber, unpeeled and diced
1 small red bell pepper, diced
8 green onions (scallions), thinly sliced
One 4^1/$_4$-ounce can chopped ripe olives, drained
^{1}/$_4$ cup pimiento-stuffed green olives, sliced
2 tablespoons chopped fresh parsley

Dressing
1 cup olive oil
2 cloves garlic, crushed
$1/2$ cup lemon juice
1 teaspoon seasoned salt
$1/2$ teaspoon pepper
1 tablespoon dried crumbled oregano

NOW

Prepare the pasta according to package directions. Rinse with cold water and drain. In a large bowl, combine pasta with the feta, tomatoes, cucumber, bell pepper, green onions, black and pimiento-stuffed olives, and parsley. Toss until well combined. Set aside.

To make the dressing, combine all the ingredients in a large jar. Cover tightly and shake vigorously until well mixed. Pour one half of the dressing over the pasta salad, and refrigerate the remainder of the dressing. Toss the salad until all items are well-coated with the dressing. Cover and refrigerate overnight or up to 3 days.

LATER

Uncover the salad, add the reserved dressing, and toss well.

Serves 10 to 12

Hen in the Hay Pasta Salad

This yummy pasta salad is perfect for family picnics and outdoor parties.

Dressing
$^1/_2$ cup salad oil
$^1/_4$ cup lemon juice
1 teaspoon dry mustard
2 cloves garlic, minced
1 teaspoon Italian herb seasoning
1 teaspoon salt
Pepper

Salad
1 pound fettuccine
2 whole boneless chicken breasts (1$^1/_2$ to 2 pounds, total), cooked and
    shredded
$^1/_2$ cup finely chopped parsley
$^1/_2$ cup freshly grated Parmesan cheese
4 ounces sliced Genoa or hard salami, cut in strips
1 cup frozen petite peas, thawed
1 pint cherry tomatoes

NOW

In a large jar, combine the oil, lemon juice, mustard, garlic, Italian seasoning, salt, and pepper to taste. Cover and shake vigorously until well combined. Refrigerate for at least 30 minutes or up to 3 days.

Prepare the pasta according to package directions. Rinse with cold water and drain. In a large bowl, combine the chicken, fettuccine, parsley,

Parmesan, salami, peas, and tomatoes. Toss with the dressing. Cover and refrigerate for several hours or up to 5 days.

LATER

Uncover the salad, and toss thoroughly.

Serves 6

Vegetable Rice Ring

The crunchy, colorful vegetables combine with the marinated rice to make a superb dish.

NOW
2 cups cooked white rice
$1/2$ cup Italian dressing
$1/2$ cup mayonnaise
1 cup sliced radishes
1 medium cucumber (skin on), seeded and finely chopped
2 small tomatoes, peeled, seeded, and finely chopped
1 medium green bell pepper coarsely chopped
1 cup finely chopped celery
$1/4$ cup thinly sliced green onions (scallions)

LATER
Large lettuce leaves to cover platter
1 pint cherry tomatoes

NOW

In a medium bowl, combine the cooked rice and Italian dressing. Cover and refrigerate for 3 hours or overnight.

Spray a $5\frac{1}{2}$-cup ring mold with vegetable spray, and set aside. Add the mayonnaise to the rice mixture, and stir until well combined. Fold in the radishes, cucumber, tomatoes, bell pepper, celery, and green onions. Transfer the mixture to the prepared mold, smoothing the top with a rubber spatula. Cover and refrigerate for 2 to 3 hours or overnight.

LATER

Cover a serving platter with the lettuce leaves. Unmold the rice ring onto the bed of lettuce. Fill the center of the ring with the cherry tomatoes.

Serves 8 to 10

Cucumber-Lime Mold

This salad is light and refreshing, and thanks to the cucumber, it has a delightful crunch.

One 3-ounce package lime Jell-O
$\frac{3}{4}$ cup boiling water
$\frac{3}{4}$ cup cream cheese (6 ounces), softened
1 cup mayonnaise
1 teaspoon prepared horseradish

¼ teaspoon salt

2 tablespoons lemon juice

1 cup diced cucumber

¼ cup green onions (scallions), minced

NOW

In a medium bowl, dissolve the Jell-O in the boiling water. Add the cream cheese, mayonnaise, horseradish, and salt. Beat with an electric mixer on medium speed until smooth. Then beat in the lemon juice.

Cover and refrigerate the Jell-O mixture for 20 to 30 minutes, until it has the consistency of egg whites. Remove it from the refrigerator, and stir in the cucumber and green onions.

Spray a 3-cup mold (or 6 individual molds) with vegetable spray. Transfer the mixture to the mold(s). Refrigerate for about 2 hours, until well set, or up to 3 days.

LATER

Unmold and serve cold.

TIP Make this in a ring-shaped mold and fill the center with crab, shrimp, or tuna salad to make a wonderful luncheon meal.

Serves 6 to 8

✳ Molded Beet Salad

At first glance, you couldn't imagine making this recipe—but it has turned out to be one of our favorites! We often pair it with Party Salad for Ten (page 73). Be sure to make it at least the day before you plan to serve it.

NOW
One 15-ounce can shoestring beets
One 3-ounce package lemon Jell-O
¼ cup sugar
¼ cup red wine vinegar
1 tablespoon prepared horseradish

LATER
1 cup mayonnaise
1 tablespoon red wine vinegar
Large red-leaf lettuce leaves, to cover the platter

NOW

Spray a 3-cup mold or 9 x 9-inch baking dish with vegetable spray, and set aside. Drain the beets, reserving the juice. Measure the beet juice, and add enough water to make 1½ cups liquid. Pour the liquid into a small skillet over high heat, and bring to boil. Remove from heat, and add the Jell-O, sugar, vinegar, and horseradish. Gently stir until the Jell-O and sugar have dissolved. In a medium bowl, combine the Jell-O mixture with the beets. Transfer to the prepared mold. Refrigerate overnight or up to 1 week.

LATER

In a small bowl, whisk together the mayonnaise and the vinegar until well combined. Cover a serving platter with the lettuce leaves. Unmold the salad onto the bed of lettuce, and serve with the mayonnaise dressing on the side.

TIP   We usually double this recipe to fill a 6-cup mold or a 9 x 13-inch baking dish.

Serves 6

Frozen Raspberry Salad

A holiday tradition in our home, this salad is so popular that we often double the recipe.

NOW

10 ounces frozen raspberries, thawed

6 ounces miniature marshmallows

1 cup crushed unsweetened pineapple, drained

3 ounces cream cheese, softened

2 tablespoons mayonnaise

1 cup heavy cream

$1/3$ cup sugar

LATER

9 to 12 lettuce leaves

NOW

Spray a 9 x 9-inch baking dish with vegetable spray, and set aside. Drain the raspberries, reserving the liquid. In a large bowl, combine the raspberries, marshmallows, and pineapple. In a small bowl, beat the cream cheese, mayonnaise, and 2 tablespoons of the reserved raspberry juice with an electric mixer. Stir the cream cheese mixture into the marshmallow mixture, and set aside.

In a medium bowl, whip the cream and beat in the sugar. Fold the whipped cream into the marshmallow mixture, gently mixing until well combined. Transfer to the prepared dish, smoothing the top with a rubber spatula. Cover tightly and freeze overnight or up to 3 months.

LATER

Remove the dish from the freezer, and let it sit, covered, for 20 minutes. Uncover the salad and cut it into squares. Serve on lettuce leaves.

 TIP If you double this recipe, freeze it in a 9 x 13-inch baking dish.

Serves 9 to 12

Lemon Pineapple Ring

This is a cool and very refreshing salad for a luncheon.

> One 6-ounce package lemon Jell-O
> 2 cups boiling water
> 1 pint lemon sherbet
> One 8-ounce can unsweetened crushed pineapple, undrained
> 1½ cups small-curd cottage cheese

NOW

In a large bowl, dissolve the Jell-O in the boiling water. Add the sherbet a spoonful at a time, stirring until melted. Stir in the pineapple and its liquid, and refrigerate until it's partially set, about 1 hour.

Spray a 6½-cup mold with vegetable spray, and set aside. Fold the cottage cheese into the Jell-O mixture. Transfer to the prepared mold, smoothing

the top with a rubber spatula. Refrigerate until set, about 5 hours, or up to
1 week.

LATER

Carefully unmold the salad onto a serving platter.

TIP Make this in a ring-shaped mold, and fill the center with fresh raspberries or fresh strawberries.

Serves 8 to 10

Orange Sunshine Salad

A sweet, smooth side salad—so refreshing!

One 6-ounce package orange Jell-O
1 cup boiling water
Two 15-ounce cans mandarin oranges, liquid reserved
2 cups sour cream
1 pint orange sherbet, softened
One 15-ounce can unsweetened crushed pineapple, drained well
2 cups unsweetened flaked coconut

In a medium bowl, dissolve the Jell-O in the boiling water. Add 1 cup of the reserved mandarin orange liquid, and refrigerate until the mixture begins to thicken, about 20 minutes.

Spray a 9 x 13-inch baking dish with vegetable spray, and set aside. Add the sour cream and sherbet to the thickened Jell-O mixture, and beat until thick and foamy. Stir in the pineapple and mandarin oranges. Pour into the prepared dish and top with the coconut. Cover and freeze for up to 1 month.

LATER

Remove from the freezer, and let sit at room temperature for 2 hours. Cut into squares and serve.

Serves 12 to 15

Yummy Fruit Dressing

Don't cringe when you read the ingredients! This dressing makes fresh fruit taste heavenly. It's also great served on the side of any molded salad.

> 1 cup marshmallow crème or Marshmallow Fluff
> 1 cup mayonnaise
> 1 teaspoon ground ginger
> 2 teaspoons grated orange zest

NOW

In a medium bowl, combine all the ingredients, and mix well. Transfer to an airtight container, and refrigerate for up to 2 weeks.

LATER

Mix well before serving cold.

Makes about 2 cups dressing

✳ Dressing for Fruit Salad

This perky dressing for fruit is distinctively different. Dress up a fruit salad and serve it with Chicken Supreme (page 157) or Sunday Strata (page 193).

1/2 cup sugar
1 teaspoon salt
1 teaspoon dry mustard
1 teaspoon celery seed
1 teaspoon paprika
1 teaspoon finely grated onion
1 cup olive oil
1/4 cup distilled white vinegar (or you can use cider vinegar)

NOW

In a medium bowl, combine the sugar, salt, dry mustard, celery seed, and paprika. Mix well, and add the onion. Next, add the oil and vinegar a little bit at a time, beating constantly with a whisk until well combined. Transfer to an airtight container, and refrigerate for up to 2 weeks.

LATER

Mix well before serving cold.

TIP Try 2 or 3 tablespoons of this dressing over fresh grapefruit segments.

Makes 1 3/4 cups dressing

Macaroon Sauce for Fruit Salad

Serve this on the side with a bowl of fresh fruit. You'll be licking your fingers!

2 cups sour cream
6 soft coconut macaroons, crumbled
¼ cup firmly packed dark brown sugar

NOW

Combine all the ingredients in a medium bowl, and mix well. Transfer to an airtight container, and refrigerate for 3 hours up to 1 week.

LATER

Mix well before serving cold.

Makes about 3 cups dressing

Crimson Dressing

This dressing is an absolute winner when served on your favorite green salad. It also works well without the cheese.

1 cup vegetable oil
$1/2$ cup firmly packed dark brown sugar
$1/2$ cup ketchup
$1/2$ cup water
$1/2$ cup distilled white vinegar
1 tablespoon lemon juice
$1/4$ medium red onion, very finely chopped
1 clove garlic, minced
$1/2$ teaspoon salt
$1/4$ teaspoon pepper
4 ounces Roquefort or blue cheese, crumbled (1 cup)

NOW

In a small bowl, whisk together the oil, brown sugar, ketchup, water, vinegar, lemon juice, onion, garlic, salt, and pepper until well blended. Gently stir in the cheese. Cover and refrigerate for at least 3 hours or up to 2 weeks.

LATER

Mix well before serving.

Makes about 3 cups dressing

Tennessee Garlic Dressing

If you like garlic, this dressing is it!

4 eggs *(see the Note on page 86 about the use of raw eggs)*
1 teaspoon salt
1 teaspoon dry mustard
4 cups vegetable oil
$\frac{1}{4}$ cup lemon juice
$\frac{1}{4}$ cup white wine vinegar
4 eggs, hard-cooked and finely minced
4 cloves garlic, minced
2 tablespoons finely chopped parsley
4 green onions (scallions), finely chopped
1 cup finely chopped celery

NOW

Put the raw eggs in a blender, and beat on low speed until well combined. Add the salt and mustard, and mix well. Continue blending on low speed, and very slowly drizzle in the oil. Add the lemon juice and vinegar, and mix well. Blend in the hard-cooked eggs, garlic, parsley, onions, and celery until well mixed. Transfer to an airtight container, and refrigerate for 2 days or up to 2 weeks.

LATER

Mix well before serving.

Makes about 1 quart

Harbor Dressing

This is a dressing everyone seems to love, and it goes with most meals.

1½ cups mayonnaise
1 cup sour cream
½ cup buttermilk
⅔ cup milk
1 tablespoon garlic salt
½ teaspoon pepper
½ cup freshly grated Parmesan
3 tablespoons white wine vinegar

NOW
Combine all the ingredients in a blender, and blend until smooth.
Transfer to an airtight container, and refrigerate for 2 hours or up to
2 weeks.

LATER
Mix well before serving.

TIP This dressing is delicious on a green salad with lots of colorful vegetables.

Makes about 3 cups dressing

Grand Roquefort Salad Dressing

We always keep this in the refrigerator, so we have it on hand for salads.

2 cups mayonnaise
1 cup sour cream
2 tablespoons lemon juice
2 tablespoons white wine vinegar
1 teaspoon salt
1 teaspoon Worcestershire sauce
$1/4$ teaspoon pepper
$1/2$ cup finely chopped green onions (scallions)
2 cloves garlic, minced
2 drops of hot pepper sauce
4 ounces Roquefort or blue cheese, crumbled (1 cup)

NOW
Combine all the ingredients in a medium bowl, and mix well. The dressing should be creamy and somewhat thick. Transfer to an airtight container, and refrigerate for 2 hours or up to 2 weeks.

LATER
Mix well before serving.

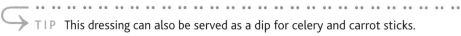

TIP This dressing can also be served as a dip for celery and carrot sticks.

Makes about 1 quart

Garlic Blue Cheese Dressing

Our version of this extraordinarily delicious dressing.

8 ounces blue cheese, crumbled (2 cups)
2 cups salad oil
$1/4$ cup olive oil
1 teaspoon salt
2 teaspoons pepper
2 tablespoons Worcestershire sauce
2 eggs, well beaten *(see the Note on page 86 about the use of raw eggs)*
2 tablespoons lemon juice
4 cloves garlic, minced

NOW

Beat the blue cheese, salad oil, and olive oil until well combined. Add the salt, pepper, and Worcestershire sauce, and mix well. Add the eggs, and mix well. Add the lemon juice and garlic, mix thoroughly, and transfer to an airtight container. Refrigerate overnight or up to 1 week.

LATER

Mix well before serving.

Makes about $3^{1}/_{2}$ cups dressing

Sweet Garlic Dressing

Few garlic dressings have a sweet flavor like this one.

1/4 cup sugar
1/2 teaspoon salt
1 large clove garlic, crushed
1/4 teaspoon white pepper
1/4 cup salad oil
1/4 cup distilled white vinegar

NOW
In a small bowl, combine all the ingredients, mixing until the sugar has dissolved. Transfer to an airtight container, and refrigerate 2 hours or up to 2 weeks.

LATER
Mix well before serving.

TIP This dressing is great on sliced tomatoes topped with fresh tarragon, or any fresh herb of your choice.

Makes about 2/3 cup dressing

✳ My Favorite French Dressing

This dressing is an oldie but a goodie—a tried-and-true original from the first **Make It Now, Bake It Later!**

2 cups olive oil or salad oil
$1/2$ cup garlic-flavor red wine vinegar
2 teaspoons salt
2 teaspoons freshly ground black pepper
2 teaspoons yellow mustard
2 teaspoons Worcestershire sauce
1 clove garlic, minced, optional

NOW

In a medium bowl, beat all the ingredients together until well combined. Transfer to an airtight container, and refrigerate for up to 2 weeks.

LATER

Mix well before serving.

TIP For Roquefort or blue cheese dressing, just add the desired amount of crumbled cheese and beat with the other ingredients.

Makes about $2^3/4$ cups dressing

Feature Attractions

The main course is the "feature attraction" of your dinner or party—the centerpiece of the meal. It is also where the *Make It Now, Bake It Later!* philosophy really delivers. The "work" part of your meal will have been done hours earlier, so your enjoyment of your own party or family dinner will be enormous.

If you're having a party, be sure to plan out the main course at least several days ahead of time. Think about what dish will go best with your event. Will the party be fun and lively or elegant and sophisticated? Will it be a small party where you will serve from the head of the table, or will it be a buffet where you'll have lots of condiments and sides for a wonderful curry or Mexican meal? Browse through our recipes to find great ideas—we have some terrific party dishes in the next few pages, and every one of them can be made hours, if not days, in advance. The last few recipes in this section will also provide the centerpieces for some wonderful brunches.

And what if you're *attending* a potluck where you have to bring a dish? Well, nothing could be easier to bring than a make-ahead feature attraction. There'll be no scrambling on the day of the party! Just pick a dish that goes well with the theme of the event, make it a day or two ahead of time, and carry it with you to the party to bake or prepare. This will free up plenty of time for you to just relax before the fun begins.

But most of all, make-ahead main courses are perfect for a quiet night at home with your family. In fact, if you make several main dishes on a Sunday afternoon (or another night of the week), you could have a week's worth of delicious and satisfying dinners all ready to go. Your family will be left wondering how you did it!

Lasagna Lollapalooza

There are many types of lasagna, but this one has a rich, wonderful flavor. It's laden with cheese and doesn't have too much pasta. Our friends actually ask us to make extras (for them!) when we make our own.

2 pounds sausage meat
1 pound ground beef
2 tablespoons dried basil
1¼ teaspoons salt
One 28-ounce can crushed tomatoes
One 12-ounce can tomato paste
2 cloves garlic, crushed
8 lasagna noodles
One 32-ounce container small-curd cottage cheese
1 cup grated Parmesan
3 tablespoons minced parsley, optional
3 eggs, lightly beaten
2 teaspoons salt
1 teaspoon pepper
1 pound mozzarella cheese, grated (4 cups)

NOW

Grease a 9 x 13-inch baking dish and set aside. In a large, heavy skillet over medium-high heat, brown the sausage and ground beef, crumbling it into small bits as it cooks. Drain off and discard the fat. Add the basil, salt, crushed tomatoes, tomato paste, and garlic. Bring to a boil, uncovered. Reduce heat to low, and simmer, stirring occasionally, for 30 to 40 minutes, until the sauce is very thick. Remove from heat, and set aside.

Cook the noodles until al dente according to the package directions. Drain the noodles, rinse in cold water, and set aside. In a medium bowl, combine the cottage cheese, Parmesan, parsley (if using), eggs, salt, and pepper, and mix well. Set aside.

Place half of the cooked noodles on the bottom of the prepared baking dish, overlapping slightly. Spread half of the cottage cheese mixture evenly over the noodles. Layer half the mozzarella and then half the meat sauce on top. Repeat the layers. Cover well and refrigerate up to 3 days, or freeze for up to 3 months.

LATER

If frozen, allow the lasagna to thaw overnight in the refrigerator. Preheat the oven to 375°F. Bake, uncovered, for 35 to 45 minutes, until hot and bubbly. Remove from the oven and let it sit for 15 to 20 minutes before serving.

Serves 8 to 10

Spaghetti Sauce

Our recipe has abundant herbs in a thick tomato sauce. You can almost smell the flavors of Tuscany.

NOW

1 pound ground beef

1 pound Italian sausage meat

3 tablespoons dried basil

3 tablespoons dried crumbled oregano

1 tablespoon dried crumbled sage

1 bay leaf

1 tablespoon dried thyme

1 tablespoon dried marjoram

1 tablespoon Italian seasoning

1 teaspoon salt

$1/2$ teaspoon pepper

1 cup red wine

1 medium yellow onion, finely chopped

2 cloves garlic, minced

One 28-ounce can crushed tomatoes

One 30-ounce can tomato sauce

One 6-ounce can tomato paste

LATER

2 pounds pasta of your choice, prepared according to the package directions

NOW

In a large, heavy skillet over medium-high heat, brown the beef and sausage, crumbling it into small bits as it cooks. Pour off the fat as it accumulates. Add the basil, oregano, sage, bay leaf, thyme, marjoram,

Italian seasoning, salt, pepper, wine, onion, and garlic, along with the crushed tomatoes, tomato sauce, and tomato paste, and mix well. Bring to a boil, uncovered. Reduce heat to low, and simmer for about 1 hour, stirring occasionally, until the sauce is thick. Remove from heat and let it cool. Transfer to an airtight container and refrigerate for up to 5 days, or freeze for up to 3 months.

LATER

If frozen, allow the sauce to thaw overnight in the refrigerator. Reheat the mixture in a large cooking pot over medium heat, adding a little water, if necessary, to moisten it. Serve over your favorite pasta.

Serves 8

Ranch Hand Request

This dish is hearty and very easy to make, especially since most of the ingredients come in cans.

> 1 pound very lean ground beef
> 1 large yellow onion, finely chopped
> One 8-ounce can tomato sauce
> 2 teaspoons garlic salt
> $1/4$ teaspoon freshly ground black pepper
> 1 package ($1^{1}/_{2}$ ounces) spaghetti sauce seasoning mix
> One 16-ounce can red kidney beans
> One 4-ounce can mushroom pieces, drained

One 4-ounce can diced chiles
2 cups grated sharp cheddar cheese, divided
1 cup crushed Fritos (preferred) or tortilla chips
1 tablespoon melted butter

NOW

Grease a 2-quart baking dish, and set aside. In a large, heavy skillet over medium-high heat, brown the beef, crumbling it into small bits as it cooks. Drain it well, discarding the fat. Add the onion, tomato sauce, garlic salt, pepper, and spaghetti seasoning. Reduce the heat to low, and simmer, covered, for 10 minutes. Add the beans, mushrooms, and chiles. Add 1 cup of the cheese, and mix well. Remove from heat, and transfer to the prepared baking dish. Top with the remaining 1 cup cheese.

In a small bowl, toss together the crushed chips and melted butter. Spread over the top of the casserole. Cover and refrigerate for 3 hours or up to 2 days.

LATER

Remove the casserole from the refrigerator, and let it sit for 20 to 30 minutes. Preheat the oven to 350°F. Bake for 30 minutes, uncover and bake until hot and bubbly, about 15 minutes more.

Serves 4 to 6

Super Nacho Feast

This is very popular—and great fun—as a dinner centerpiece. Forks aren't even necessary!

NOW
1¹/₂ pounds ground beef
1 package (1¹/₄ ounces) taco seasoning
Two 15-ounce cans refried beans
One 4-ounce can chopped green chiles
2 cups grated cheddar-jack cheese (or use cheddar or Monterey Jack cheese, or a combination)
1 cup taco sauce

LATER
1 cup sour cream
1 cup guacamole or chopped avocado
1 cup chopped radishes
1 cup chopped black olives
1 cup chopped fresh tomatoes
1 cup salsa
1 cup chopped green onions (scallions)
Tortilla or corn chips, for scooping

NOW
Lightly grease a 9 x 13-inch baking dish with vegetable cooking spray, and set aside. In a large, heavy skillet over medium-high heat, brown the beef, crumbling it as it cooks. Drain off the fat as it accumulates. Add the taco seasoning and mix well. Remove from heat and set aside.

Spread the refried beans in a layer on the bottom of the prepared baking dish, and top with the beef. Next, sprinkle the chopped chiles over the beef. Cover with a layer of the cheese, and drizzle the taco sauce on top. Cover, and refrigerate for several hours or up to 2 days.

LATER

Preheat the oven to 350°F. Bake, uncovered, for 30 minutes, until the cheese has melted and it is bubbly around the edges. Remove from the oven, and let the dip sit for 10 minutes before serving.

With the sour cream, guacamole, radishes, black olives, tomatoes, salsa, and green onions, *either* spread a layer of each on top of the baked nacho dip *or* serve them in side dishes. Either way, it's great! Serve with tortilla or corn chips.

Serves 6 to 8

# Teen Mix

This chili has been one of Scott's favorite meals since he was a child.

NOW

4 slices bacon, cut into bite-sized pieces
1 large yellow onion, finely chopped
2 pounds very lean ground beef
One 28-ounce can baked beans, undrained
1 tablespoon Worcestershire sauce
One 28-ounce can crushed tomatoes, undrained
1 tablespoon garlic salt
1 heaping teaspoon sugar
1 teaspoon salt
1 teaspoon pepper

LATER

Hamburger buns, optional

NOW

In a large cooking pot over medium heat, cook the bacon with the onion until the bacon becomes clear and soft. (Do not brown the bacon.) Add the ground beef, and continue cooking until it has browned slightly. Drain off the excess fat.

Add the beans, Worcestershire sauce, tomatoes, garlic salt, sugar, salt, and pepper. Stir gently to combine, and reduce heat to low. Cover, and simmer the chili for 1 hour, stirring occasionally. Remove from heat, and allow to cool. Transfer to an airtight container, and refrigerate for up to 5 days.

LATER

In a large cooking pot over medium heat, reheat the chili, stirring frequently. Serve in bowls or on toasted hamburger buns.

Serves 4 to 6

Manhattan Spaghetti Pie

Our fabulous editor, Jennifer Lang, makes this universally appealing dish, puts it in a disposable aluminum baking pan, and brings it to friends' homes when they have a newborn baby!

NOW
$^1/_2$ pound thin spaghetti
6 tablespoons butter ($^3/_4$ stick), divided
1 cup grated Parmesan cheese
One 15-ounce container whole milk ricotta cheese
1 medium yellow onion, finely chopped
$^1/_2$ pound mushrooms, sliced, optional
$^1/_2$ medium green bell pepper, finely diced, optional
2 cloves garlic, passed through a garlic press
2 pounds ground beef
2 tablespoons Italian herb seasoning
One 6-ounce can tomato paste
One 28-ounce can crushed tomatoes

LATER

8 ounces mozzarella cheese, grated (2 cups)

NOW

Grease a 9 x 13-inch baking dish, and set aside. Cook the spaghetti according to the package directions, and drain. Put 4 tablespoons of the butter into the hot pot used to boil the spaghetti, and return the spaghetti to the pot. Add the Parmesan and mix until the butter melts. Pour the spaghetti mixture into the prepared baking dish and spread it across the bottom and up the sides of the dish, as if making a crust. Spread the ricotta on top of the spaghetti mixture, and set aside.

In a large skillet over medium-high heat, cook the onion and the mushrooms and bell pepper (if you choose to use them) with the garlic in the remaining 2 tablespoons butter for about 3 minutes. Add the ground beef and brown it, crumbling it into small bits as it cooks. Pour off the fat as it accumulates. Mix in the Italian seasoning, tomato paste, and crushed tomatoes, and cook until heated through, stirring occasionally. Spoon the ground beef mixture on top of the ricotta cheese. Cover and refrigerate for up to 24 hours, or freeze for up to 3 months.

LATER

If frozen, allow the pie to thaw overnight in the refrigerator. Preheat the oven to 350°F. Bake, uncovered, for about 35 minutes, until it starts to bubble around the sides. Top with the mozzarella cheese, and bake for 5 to 10 minutes more. Remove the pie from the oven, and let sit for 10 minutes before serving.

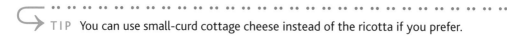

TIP You can use small-curd cottage cheese instead of the ricotta if you prefer.

Serves 8 to 10

✳ Divine Tamale Pie

Even now, more than forty years after the first Make It Now, Bake It Later! *cookbook was published, we hear from people who still serve this dish when their best friends come to visit.*

NOW

1 cup yellow cornmeal
1 cup water
One 5-ounce can evaporated milk
1 teaspoon salt
1 medium yellow onion, finely chopped
1$\frac{1}{2}$ pounds ground beef
2 tablespoons chili powder
1 tablespoon ground cumin
1 teaspoon garlic salt
Salt and pepper
One 15-ounce can cream-style corn
One 28-ounce can solid-pack tomatoes
One 6-ounce can ripe pitted olives, drained (1$\frac{1}{2}$ cups)

LATER

One package (8$\frac{1}{2}$-ounces) yellow corn muffin mix

NOW

Generously grease a 7 x 11-inch baking dish, and set aside. In a medium saucepan over medium heat, combine the cornmeal, water, evaporated milk, and salt. Cook for 5 minutes stirring constantly, until thick. Spread the cornmeal mixture evenly over the bottom of the baking dish to form a crust. Set aside to cool.

In a large skillet, cook the onion with the beef, crumbling the beef as it cooks, until all the red color is gone. Add the chili powder, cumin, and garlic salt, and mix well. Season with salt and pepper. Add the corn and tomatoes, including their juice. Carefully spoon the beef mixture on top of the cornmeal layer that is now firm and cool in the baking dish. Dot the top with the olives. Cover and refrigerate for at least 4 hours or up to 3 days.

LATER

Preheat the oven to 375°F. Prepare (but do not cook) the corn muffin mix according to the package directions. Carefully spread it on top of the beef mixture, making sure to spread to the edges. Bake, uncovered, for 20 minutes. Reduce the heat to 300°F and bake for 40 minutes more.

TIP   This dish is best if you start it a full day ahead; the meat mixture has more flavor if it stands.

Serves 6

 # *Layers*

Meat, potato, and vegetables all in one! This is a great dish to take to sick friends or new families in the neighborhood.

1 pound ground beef
3 medium carrots, peeled and sliced
3 stalks celery, sliced
1 large baking potato, peeled and sliced
1 medium yellow onion, peeled and sliced
1 small green bell pepper, finely chopped
One 4-ounce can mushrooms, drained
1 teaspoon dried basil
1 teaspoon dried parsley
$1/4$ teaspoon dried tarragon
Salt and pepper
One $10^{1}/_2$-ounce can tomato soup

NOW

Break the beef into small pieces and spread them on the bottom of a 2-quart baking dish. Make a carrot layer on top of the beef. Then, layer the celery, the potato, the onion, the bell pepper, and end with the mushrooms. Sprinkle with the basil, parsley, tarragon, salt, and pepper. Spread the soup evenly on top. Cover and refrigerate for at least 4 hours (preferably overnight) or up to 48 hours.

LATER

Preheat the oven to 350°F. Bake the casserole, covered, for 2 hours.

Serves 4

Pizza Casserole

This is a "pizza in a dish" recipe that everyone seems to love.

$^1/_2$ pound thin spaghetti noodles

2 tablespoons butter

1 pound ground beef, Italian sausage, or a combination of the two

1 medium yellow onion, finely chopped

1 teaspoon garlic salt

Salt and pepper

One 28-ounce can spaghetti sauce

One 7-ounce jar pizza sauce

$^1/_2$ pound sliced pepperoni

One 4-ounce can sliced mushrooms, drained

8 ounces mozzarella cheese, grated (2 cups)

$^1/_4$ cup grated Parmesan cheese

NOW

Grease a 9 x 13-inch ovenproof glass baking dish, and set aside. Cook the spaghetti according to the package directions, drain it, and return it to the pot. Toss the spaghetti with the butter, and transfer it to the prepared baking dish, spreading it to cover the bottom of the dish. In a medium skillet over medium-high heat, brown the meat with the onion. Stir in the garlic salt, and season the meat with the salt and pepper. Spread the meat mixture over the spaghetti.

While the meat is browning, combine the spaghetti sauce and pizza sauce in a medium bowl. Pour half of this sauce over the meat. Top with a layer of the pepperoni and then a layer of the mushrooms. Cover with the mozzarella, then the remaining sauce. Sprinkle the Parmesan on top. Cover well and refrigerate for 3 hours or up to 24 hours.

LATER

Remove the casserole from the refrigerator, and let it sit for 20 to 30 minutes. Preheat the oven to 350°F. Bake, uncovered, for 30 to 45 minutes, until bubbly.

Serves 6 to 8

 ✳ The Meal

This is a very satisfying, complete *meal in a pot.*

NOW
2 pounds lean ground beef
1 medium yellow onion, coarsely chopped
5 cups water
2 cups red wine
6 beef bouillon cubes
2 large leeks, thinly sliced
2 cups thinly sliced carrots
2 cups thinly sliced celery
One 10-ounce package frozen French-cut green beans, thawed
1 bay leaf
2 tablespoons dried basil
One 15-ounce can tomato sauce
Salt and pepper

LATER

1 cup broken spaghetti noodles
$1/2$ cup sherry, optional
$1/2$ cup grated Parmesan cheese

NOW

In large pot on medium-high heat, brown the beef, crumbling it as it cooks. Add the onion, and cook until the onion is glossy, stirring often. Drain it well, discarding the fat. Add the water, wine, bouillon cubes, leeks, carrots, celery, green beans, bay leaf, basil, and tomato sauce. Bring to a boil, and season with salt and pepper. Cover, reduce heat to low, and simmer for about 15 minutes. Remove the pot from heat and allow it to cool. Cover well and refrigerate overnight, or freeze for up to 3 months.

LATER

If frozen, allow the pot to thaw overnight in the refrigerator. Bring it to boil in a large pot over medium-high heat. Reduce the heat to low and add the spaghetti pieces. Simmer for 15 to 20 minutes, until the spaghetti is thoroughly cooked. Remove the casserole from heat, and stir in the sherry if desired. Serve with the Parmesan on the side.

Serves 8

Mimi's Famous Pot Roast

Ann's sister in Half Moon Bay, California, makes this wonderful pot roast.

NOW

1 beef roast (about 4 to 4^1/$_2$ pounds)

All-purpose flour

Salt and pepper

^{1}/$_4$ cup butter (^{1}/$_2$ stick)

2 cloves garlic, minced

One 28-ounce can crushed tomatoes

Two 10^3/$_4$-ounce cans beef consommé (2^2/$_3$ cups)

1 cup red wine

LATER

3 large potatoes, cut into small cubes (peeled or unpeeled, as you prefer)

^{1}/$_2$ pound baby carrots

3 medium stalks celery, sliced

2 tablespoons cornstarch

^{1}/$_2$ cup water

NOW

Preheat the oven to 325°F. Dust the roast generously with flour, salt, and pepper, and set aside. In a large, ovenproof pot with a lid, melt the butter over medium-high heat. Add the dusted roast and brown it, turning to brown all sides. Add the garlic, tomatoes, consommé, and wine, and bring to boil. Remove from heat, cover the pot, and bake the roast for 2 hours. Remove from the oven, allow the roast to cool, and refrigerate it, covered, overnight or up to 3 days.

Preheat the oven to 350°F. Bring the roast and its cooking liquid to a boil over medium-high heat, and add the potatoes, carrots, and celery. Cover, and bake for 1 hour. Remove the pot from the oven, and transfer the roast and vegetables to a serving platter. Quickly combine the cornstarch and water, and add it to the hot liquid remaining in the pot. Stir until the gravy is smooth and thick. Serve it on the side.

Serves 6 to 8

Kamaaina Beef

Kamaaina *is a Hawaiian word that means "someone in the know, someone who knows the secrets." You'll be just such an insider once you try this delicious dish.*

NOW

2 tablespoons olive oil

2 pounds top round or good stew meat, cut into bite-sized pieces

One 14-ounce can beef broth ($1^3/_4$ cups)

1 cup ketchup

$1/_2$ cup firmly packed dark brown sugar

1 bay leaf

1 tablespoon Worcestershire sauce

1 clove garlic, minced

2 tablespoons red wine vinegar

$1/_4$ cup raisins or currants

1 small yellow onion, finely chopped

1 cup sliced fresh mushrooms

1 heaping teaspoon curry powder

LATER

Cornstarch, if needed

3 cups cooked white rice

6 to 8 slices bacon, fried crisp and crumbled (1 cup)

1 cup chopped green onions (scallions)

1 cup shredded unsweetened coconut

1 cup chopped macadamia nuts

NOW

Preheat the oven to 400°F. Combine the oil and the beef in a large baking pan with a tight-fitting lid, and bake it for 30 minutes. Reduce the heat to 350°F, add the beef broth, and bake for 1 hour more. Remove from the heat, and set aside.

In a medium bowl, combine the ketchup, brown sugar, bay leaf, Worcestershire sauce, garlic, vinegar, raisins, onion, mushrooms, and curry powder, and mix well. Add the sauce to the beef in the baking pan, and mix thoroughly. Allow the beef to cool, cover it, and refrigerate overnight or up to 2 days.

LATER

Preheat the oven to 350°F. Bake, covered, for 1 hour. Thicken the sauce with cornstarch, if necessary. Serve the stew on the rice with the bacon, green onions, coconut, and macadamia nuts on the side as toppings.

Serves 6

County Kilkenny Beef and Dumplings

This delicious stew will get you happily through any "dark and stormy night."

NOW

2 pounds round steak, cut into 1-inch cubes
2 medium yellow onions, thinly sliced
1 bay leaf
One 10³/₄-ounce can cream of chicken soup
One 10³/₄-ounce can cream of mushroom soup
One 4-ounce can mushrooms, drained
1 tablespoon Worcestershire sauce
¹/₃ cup all-purpose flour

LATER

1 cup all-purpose flour
1¹/₂ teaspoons baking powder
¹/₂ teaspoon salt
1 egg
¹/₃ cup milk
2 tablespoons vegetable oil
2 tablespoons chopped parsley
¹/₂ teaspoon dried crumbled sage
One 10-ounce package frozen peas, thawed

NOW

Preheat the oven to 350°F. Put the steak in a 3-quart baking dish with a lid. Cover with the onions and the bay leaf, and set aside. In a medium bowl, combine the soups, mushrooms, Worcestershire sauce, and flour, mix well, and pour over the onions. Bake 1 hour, covered. Cool and refrigerate overnight or up to 3 days.

Remove the stew from the refrigerator, and let it sit for 20 to 30 minutes. Preheat the oven to 350°F. Bake for 1 hour, covered, until it's hot and bubbly.

While the stew is baking, prepare the parsley dumplings. In a small bowl, combine the flour, baking powder, and salt. In a medium bowl, combine the egg, milk, oil, parsley, and sage, and mix well. Add the flour mixture, stirring only until the dry ingredients are moistened, and set aside.

Remove the stew from oven, and increase the heat to 400°F. Remove and discard the bay leaf and put the peas on top of the stew. Drop the dumpling mixture into the hot stew by the teaspoonful. Cover and bake for 20 to 25 minutes more.

Serves 6

 Beef Brisket

This entrée is unique because it can be served either hot or cold.

NOW
One 16-ounce can tomato sauce
$1/4$ cup chopped yellow onion
One 4-ounce can mushrooms, including their liquid
1 beef brisket (3 to 4 pounds)
1 package (1 ounce) dehydrated onion soup mix

LATER
4 cups cooked rice

NOW

Preheat the oven to 325°F. In a medium bowl, combine the tomato sauce with the onion. Pour half of this mixture into the bottom of a roasting pan large enough to accommodate the brisket. Add the mushrooms with their liquid, and place the beef on top of the mushrooms. Sprinkle the soup mix on the beef, and pour the remaining tomato mixture on top. Bake, covered, for 3 hours, basting occasionally. Remove the brisket from the oven, and allow it to cool. Cover well, and refrigerate overnight.

LATER

Serve the brisket cold and thinly sliced, or reheat it, covered, at 300°F for 30 to 40 minutes. Serve with the sauce over the rice.

Serves 8 or more

✳ Marinade for Beef

This truly is one of the most versatile recipes in the book. We use it all the time on flank steak.

> ¹/₂ cup vegetable oil
> ¹/₂ cup soy sauce
> ¹/₂ cup red wine
> 1 tablespoon lemon juice
> 2 cloves garlic, minced
> ¹/₂ teaspoon pepper
> ¹/₄ teaspoon salt
> 1 tablespoon sugar

NOW

In a medium bowl, combine all the ingredients, and mix well. Use it to marinate beef, covered, in the refrigerator for 1 hour or overnight.

LATER

Drain off the marinade and cook the beef as you desire.

TIP Put the steak in a large, airtight plastic bag and pour the marinade over the meat. Close securely and refrigerate. (We lay the bag flat on a dish in case it leaks.) Flip the bag over once or twice to spread around the marinade. Or freeze the steak in the marinade for up to 3 months. Thaw overnight in the refrigerator before cooking.

Makes enough marinade for 4 to 5 pounds beef

Cinco de Mayo Beef

This recipe-for-a-crowd can also be used in tacos, enchiladas, or in any dish you want.

NOW

1 beef roast or pork roast (about 5 pounds)
1 medium yellow onion, finely chopped
1 tablespoon minced garlic
One 4-ounce can diced green chiles
1 tablespoon ground cumin
1 package (1$^1/_4$ ounces) taco seasoning
1 teaspoon seasoned salt
1 cup salsa

LATER

Beef broth, if needed
Warm flour tortillas
A variety of the following:
   1 cup sour cream, divided
   1 cup grated Monterey Jack cheese
   1 cup chopped green onions (scallions)
   1 cup chopped cilantro
   1 cup chopped tomatoes
   1 cup shredded lettuce
   1 cup corn chips crushed
   1 cup chopped ripe olives
   1 cup guacamole or sliced avocados
   1 cup salsa

NOW

Preheat the oven to 300°F. Spray a large ovenproof pot (with a tight-fitting lid) with vegetable cooking spray. Place the roast inside and cover. (Do *not* add anything else to the meat or the pot.) Bake, covered, for 4 to 5 hours, until the meat is tender. Remove the meat from the pan, leaving any accumulated liquid, allow it to cool, and then shred it. Return the shredded meat to the pot, and add the onions, garlic, chiles, cumin, taco seasoning, seasoned salt, and salsa. Stir thoroughly. Cover and refrigerate for up to 1 week, or freeze for up to 3 months.

LATER

If frozen, allow the meat mixture to thaw overnight in the refrigerator. Reheat in a large pot on low heat, stirring frequently, until thoroughly warmed. Add some beef broth if necessary to moisten it. Serve with warm flour tortillas and a selection of the toppings on the side—the more, the better!

Serves up to 24

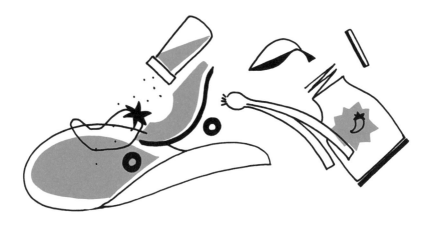

Tijuana Torte

This South-of-the-Border torte is a real crowd-pleaser.

NOW
2 pounds ground beef
1 teaspoon seasoned salt
1 package (1¼ ounces) taco seasoning mix
One 15-ounce can diced tomatoes, drained and coarsely chopped
One 15-ounce can tomato sauce
One 4-ounce can diced green chiles
One 8-ounce container ricotta or cottage cheese
2 eggs, lightly beaten
10 corn tortillas, each cut into 6 wedges
1 cup salsa
16 ounces Monterey Jack cheese, grated (4 cups)

LATER
Salsa Linda (page 60) or salsa of your choice, for serving

NOW

Grease a 9 x 13-inch baking dish, and set aside. In a large, heavy skillet over medium-high heat, brown the beef, crumbling it as it cooks. Pour off any fat as it accumulates. Add the seasoned salt, taco seasoning mix, diced tomatoes, tomato sauce, and chiles, and mix well. Reduce the heat to low and simmer, uncovered, stirring occasionally, for 10 minutes. Set aside.

In a medium bowl, combine the ricotta and eggs, and mix well. In another medium bowl, gently combine the tortilla wedges with the salsa until all the wedges are coated with salsa. Spread half of the meat mixture on the bottom of the prepared baking dish, followed by a layer of half of the coated tortilla wedges, and then half of the ricotta mixture. Top with 2 cups of the Monterey Jack cheese. Repeat the layers, ending with the remaining 2 cups cheese. Cover and refrigerate overnight or up to 2 days, or freeze for up to 3 months.

LATER

If frozen, allow the torte to thaw overnight in the refrigerator. Remove from the refrigerator and let it sit for 20 to 30 minutes. Preheat the oven to 375°F. Bake, covered, for 35 minutes. Remove the cover and bake for 15 minutes more, until hot and bubbly. Let it stand for 10 minutes before serving with extra salsa on the side.

TIP You can use 4 cups cooked and shredded chicken in place of the ground beef.

Serves 8 to 12

MAKE IT NOW, BAKE IT LATER!

Veal Stew with Artichokes

Easy and glamorous—for a stew, that is! This dish is terrific served over noodles or rice.

NOW

2 pounds lean boneless veal, cut into bite-sized pieces
$1/3$ cup all-purpose flour
One 10-ounce package frozen artichoke hearts, thawed
$1/4$ cup vegetable oil
1 large yellow onion, finely chopped
One 14-ounce can chicken broth ($1^3/4$ cups)
$1/2$ cup dry white wine
1 tablespoon dried basil
6 ounces thinly sliced smoked beef, cut into slivers
6 ounces Swiss cheese, grated ($1^1/2$ cups)

LATER

Chicken broth, if needed

NOW

Dust the veal in the flour, shaking off the excess flour, and set aside. Cut each artichoke heart in half, and set aside. In a large saucepan, heat the oil over medium-high heat. Add the veal and cook, stirring frequently, until well-browned. Add the onion and cook until softened. Add the broth, wine, and basil. Reduce heat to low, cover, and simmer, stirring occasionally, until the veal is tender, about 1½ hours. Add the artichokes, and cook, covered, for 5 minutes more. Stir the smoked beef and cheese into the veal mixture, and remove from heat. Allow the stew to cool, transfer it to an airtight container, and refrigerate overnight or up to 3 days.

In a large saucepan over medium heat, reheat the stew, stirring frequently. Add a little chicken broth or water to moisten it if necessary.

Serves 4

Chicken Curry

Here's a bountiful buffet table meal—the maharaja never had it so good!

NOW
Curry
3 tablespoons butter
$^1/_2$ medium yellow onion, finely chopped
$1^1/_2$ teaspoons curry powder
3 tablespoons all-purpose flour
$^3/_4$ teaspoon salt
$^3/_4$ teaspoon sugar
$^1/_4$ teaspoon ground ginger
1 cup chicken broth
1 cup milk
2 cups cooked and shredded chicken (or cooked shrimp)
1 teaspoon lemon juice

LATER
Condiments
1 cup sliced bananas, sprinkled with a little pineapple juice
1 cup chutney

1 cup chopped green onions (scallions)
1 cup chopped peanuts
1 cup raisins
1 cup crushed pineapple, drained
1 cup bacon pieces
1 cup shredded coconut
1 cup chopped celery
1 cup chopped cilantro
1 cup chopped tomatoes
1 cup grated hard-cooked egg
One 2.8-ounce can French-fried onions (1 cup)

Curry
Milk, if needed
3 cups cooked rice

NOW

Melt the butter in a large pot over low heat. Gently cook the onion and curry powder until the onion begins to soften. With a whisk, blend in the flour, salt, sugar, and ginger, and cook until the sauce is smooth and bubbly. Stir in the broth and milk, and bring to a boil for 1 minute, stirring constantly. Stir in the chicken and lemon juice, remove from heat and allow the curry to cool. Cover and refrigerate overnight or up to 3 days.

LATER

Prepare a selection of the condiments (the more, the better!), and refrigerate them in airtight containers until ready to use. In a medium saucepan over medium heat, reheat the chicken mixture, adding a little milk if it is too thick. Serve the chicken curry over rice with many colorful condiments arrayed alongside.

Serves 4 to 6

Surefire Chicken and Rice

This dish hits the spot for both guests and hungry teenagers alike. It's particularly tasty if you refrigerate it overnight. Serve it with a colorful, crunchy salad, such as Mandarin Orange Salad (page 80).

4 cups cooked and shredded chicken
3 cups finely chopped celery
One 10^3/$_4$-ounce can cream of chicken soup
One 10^3/$_4$-ounce can cream of celery soup
1^1/$_2$ cups mayonnaise
2 tablespoons lemon juice
2^2/$_3$ cups instant rice
1^1/$_2$ cups evaporated milk
One 8-ounce can sliced water chestnuts, drained and finely chopped
1 small yellow onion, finely chopped
Salt and pepper
3 cups cornflakes cereal, crushed
^{1}/$_2$ cup butter (1 stick), melted
1 cup slivered almonds, optional

NOW

Lightly grease a 9 x 13-inch baking dish, and set aside. In a large bowl, combine the chicken, celery, soups, mayonnaise, lemon juice, rice, evaporated milk, water chestnuts, and onion. Mix well, and season with salt and pepper to taste. Pour into the prepared baking dish. In a medium bowl, combine the cornflakes, butter, and almonds if desired. Mix well, and spread evenly on top of the chicken mixture. Cover well and refrigerate for at least 3 hours or overnight preferably.

LATER

Preheat the oven to 350°F. Bake the prepared casserole, covered, for 45 minutes. Remove the cover, and bake 15 minutes more, until it's lightly browned and bubbly around the edges.

Serves 8 to 10

Chicken and Broccoli

This dish is light, but don't let that keep you from serving it for dinner — it's also quite filling.

2 whole boneless chicken breasts, cooked and shredded
Two 10³/₄-ounce cans cream of chicken soup
¹/₂ cup mayonnaise
1 tablespoon lemon juice
1 teaspoon curry powder
Two 10-ounce packages frozen chopped broccoli, thawed and drained
Salt and pepper
8 ounces cheddar cheese, grated (2 cups)
2 cups Pepperidge Farm herb seasoned stuffing mix, coarsely crushed
2 tablespoons butter, melted

NOW

Grease a 9 x 13-inch baking dish, and set aside. In a large bowl, combine the chicken, soup, mayonnaise, lemon juice, curry powder, and broccoli. Season with salt and pepper to taste. Transfer to the prepared baking dish, and top with the cheese. In a medium bowl, combine the stuffing and melted butter, mixing well, and spread it over the cheese. Cover and refrigerate for 3 hours or up to 2 days.

LATER

Remove the casserole from the refrigerator and let it sit for 20 to 30 minutes. Preheat the oven to 350°F. Bake, uncovered, for 35 to 45 minutes, until the casserole is bubbly and browned on top.

Serves 6 to 8

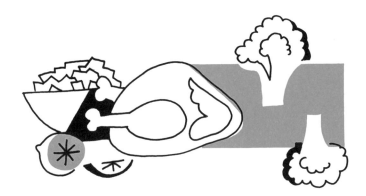

Elegant Chicken Lasagna

This dish is a classy change from typical lasagnas.

1/2 cup butter (1 stick), divided
1 pound mushrooms, sliced
1/2 cup dry white wine
1/2 teaspoon dried tarragon
Two 10-ounce packages frozen artichoke hearts, thawed and cut into bite-sized pieces
1/4 cup all-purpose flour
1/4 teaspoon pepper
1/4 teaspoon nutmeg
2 tablespoons chicken bouillon granules
2 cups half-and-half
2 cups chicken broth
Salt and white pepper
12 lasagna noodles
4 cups shredded cooked chicken or turkey
12 ounces Swiss cheese, grated (3 cups)

NOW

Spray a 9 x 13-inch baking dish with vegetable cooking spray, and set aside. Melt 1/4 cup of the butter in a medium skillet on medium heat. Add the mushrooms and cook until tender, 10 to 15 minutes. Add the wine, tarragon, and artichoke hearts. Reduce the heat to medium-low and continue cooking, stirring occasionally, until almost all the liquid has evaporated, about 15 minutes. Remove from heat and set aside.

Melt the remaining 1/4 cup butter in a medium saucepan over medium heat. Add the flour, whisking well. Stir in the pepper, nutmeg, and bouillon granules. Cook, stirring frequently, until the sauce becomes bubbly, about 5 to 10 minutes. Remove from heat, and gradually stir in the half-and-half and broth. Return the pan to the heat, and continue cooking until the sauce has thickened. Stir in the reserved mushroom mixture. Season with salt and white pepper to taste, and set aside.

Cook the noodles according to the package directions, drain them, rinse, and set aside. Spread a very thin layer of the mushroom sauce over the bottom of the prepared baking dish. Arrange one-third of the noodles evenly on top. Continue layering with one-third of the chicken, one-third of the remaining mushroom sauce, and one-third of the cheese. Repeat the layering two more times, ending with the cheese. Cover well and refrigerate overnight or up to 2 days, or freeze for up to 3 months.

LATER

If frozen, allow the lasagna to thaw overnight in the refrigerator. Preheat the oven to 350°F. Bake, uncovered, for 40 to 50 minutes, until hot and bubbly. Let it sit for 10 minutes before cutting it into squares to serve.

Serves 10 to 12

MAKE IT NOW, BAKE IT LATER!

Chicken Supreme

This is a classic casserole for any occasion, but the colors are perfect for the Thanksgiving and Christmas holidays.

4 cups shredded cooked chicken
1 package Uncle Ben's long grain and wild rice, prepared according to the package directions (about 3 cups cooked rice)
One 10¾-ounce can cream of celery soup
One 5-ounce jar diced pimientos
1 medium yellow onion, finely chopped
One 10-ounce package frozen French-cut green beans, thawed and drained
1 cup mayonnaise
One 8-ounce can water chestnuts, coarsely chopped
Salt and pepper

NOW

Lightly grease a 9 x 13-inch baking dish, and set aside. In a large bowl, combine all the ingredients, seasoning with salt and pepper to taste. Pour into the prepared baking dish. Cover and refrigerate for up to 2 days, or freeze for up to 3 months.

LATER

If frozen, allow the casserole to thaw overnight in the refrigerator. Remove from the refrigerator, and let it sit for 20 to 30 minutes (or 40 to 60 minutes if previously frozen). Preheat the oven to 350°F. Bake the casserole for 30 to 45 minutes, until bubbly.

TIP Never serve the same casserole to the same guest twice. Mother always kept a little metal box with index cards to note what she served to each guest who came over. If the person made any special comment, Mother would jot it down on that recipe's card. If the person loved a particular dish, Mother would try to serve it to them again sometime.

•• •• •• •• •• •• •• •• • •• •• •• •• • •• •• • •• •• •• •• •• •• • •• •• • •• •• •• •• ••

Serves 8 to 10

Company Casserole

This dish may seem like it has a lot of ingredients, but it has something for everyone and is universally popular.

NOW
1 pound medium-wide noodles
6 cups chicken broth
1 medium yellow onion, finely chopped
1 small green bell pepper, finely chopped
One 8-ounce can sliced mushrooms, drained
2 tablespoons butter
4 cups cooked chicken, cut into bite-sized pieces
1 cup finely diced ham
One 8-ounce can sliced ripe olives, drained
1 cup thinly sliced celery
One 2-ounce jar diced pimientos
One 10-ounce package frozen peas, thawed and drained
$1/2$ teaspoon salt
$1/4$ teaspoon pepper
1 teaspoon celery salt

One 10^3/$_4$-ounce can cream of chicken soup
One 10^3/$_4$-ounce can cream of celery soup

LATER
2 cups grated sharp cheddar cheese
2 tablespoons freshly grated Parmesan cheese
^{1}/$_2$ cup chicken broth, if needed

NOW

Grease a 9 x 13-inch baking dish, and set aside. In a large pot, cook the noodles according to the package directions using the chicken broth as the cooking liquid. Drain, transfer the noodles into a large mixing bowl, and set aside.

In a large skillet, over medium-high heat, cook the onion, bell pepper, and mushrooms in the butter until tender, about 3 to 5 minutes. Add the vegetables to the noodles, and mix well. Add the chicken, ham, olives, celery, pimientos, peas, salt, pepper, celery salt, and soups, and mix thoroughly. Pour the casserole mixture into the prepared baking dish. (It will be full.) Cover and refrigerate overnight or up to 3 days, or freeze for up to 3 months.

LATER

If frozen, allow the casserole to thaw overnight in the refrigerator. Remove from the refrigerator, and let it sit for 20 to 30 minutes. Preheat the oven to 325°F. Top the casserole with the cheeses. Uncover and bake for 1 hour, until bubbly. If the casserole looks a bit dry, sprinkle ^{1}/$_2$ cup additional chicken broth over it.

TIP We sometimes mix the casserole ingredients, halve them, bake one half, and put the other half in an 8 x 8-inch dish and freeze for another occasion.

Serves 12 to 15

White Chili

This is a very festive dish, especially since everyone can "dress up" his or her own meal. It's great served with cornbread.

NOW
1 pound dried small white beans, rinsed
6 cups chicken broth
1 tablespoon chicken bouillon granules
2 medium yellow onions, finely chopped
6 to 8 cloves garlic, minced
One 7-ounce can diced green chiles
4 teaspoons ground cumin
2 teaspoons dried crumbled oregano
1 teaspoon cayenne pepper
4 cups cooked and diced chicken

LATER
2 cups sour cream, divided
3 cups grated Monterey Jack cheese
1 cup chopped green onions (scallions)
1 cup chopped cilantro
1 cup chopped tomatoes
1 cup shredded lettuce
1 cup corn chips, crushed
1 cup chopped ripe olives
1 cup guacamole or sliced avocados
1 cup salsa

NOW

In a large pot, combine the beans, broth, and bouillon granules, and bring to a boil over medium-high heat. Reduce the heat to the lowest setting, and simmer, covered, for 2 hours. Add the onions, garlic, chiles, cumin, oregano, cayenne, and chicken. Increase the heat to low, and simmer, covered, for 30 minutes more. Remove the chili from heat, and allow it to cool. Cover and refrigerate overnight or for up to 3 days.

LATER

In a large saucepan over medium heat, reheat the chili, stirring frequently. If necessary, add a little water to moisten the mixture. When warm, add 1 cup of the sour cream and all the Monterey Jack cheese. Continue cooking just until the cheese melts, and remove from heat. In individual side dishes, serve the green onions, cilantro, tomatoes, lettuce, corn chips, olives, guacamole, salsa, and remaining 1 cup sour cream as toppings for the chili.

TIP It's fun to serve the chili in Tortilla Bowls (page 162).

Serves 6 to 8

Tortilla Bowls

Vegetable oil, for frying
6 to 8 flour tortillas

NOW

Remove the paper wrapping from an empty 28-ounce can. Clean and thoroughly dry the can. Punch four holes in the closed end, and set aside. Fill a deep fryer or deep, heavy saucepan with 2 to 3 inches oil. Heat oil until hot but not smoking. Using tongs, place one tortilla on top of the hot oil.

Hold the prepared can with the tongs, closed-end down. Push the can down onto the center of the tortilla, forcing the center of the tortilla toward the bottom of the pan. (The sides of the tortilla will float upward around the can.) *Be very careful of the hot oil!*

Deep-fry the tortilla in this manner just until it begins to stiffen and brown. Tilt the can, and carefully remove the can and the shaped tortilla, remembering that the hot oil in the can will drain out of the holes as you pull it out. Drain the tortilla bowl upside down on paper towels. Repeat for each tortilla.

Allow the tortilla bowls to cool, and store them in an airtight container if you won't use them in a few hours. They will keep 2 days at room temperature. They can be re-crisped by placing them on a baking sheet and heating them in a preheated 400°F oven. Watch them carefully so that they do not burn.

LATER

Fill the bowls with White Chili (page 160) or another filling of your choice and serve hot.

Makes 6 to 8 tortilla bowls

✳ No Work Chicken

This easy marinade is so good, and the chicken improves the longer it marinates.

2 whole chicken breasts, skinned, split, and boned
¹/₂ cup honey
¹/₂ cup Dijon mustard
1 tablespoon curry powder
2 tablespoons soy sauce

NOW

Place the chicken breast halves in a baking dish that will fit them snugly in one layer. In a small bowl, make the sauce by combining the honey, mustard, curry powder, and soy sauce, and mix well. Pour the sauce over the chicken, cover, and refrigerate for 6 hours or up to 24 hours.

LATER

Preheat the oven to 350°F. Turn the chicken pieces, and bake, covered, for 1 hour. Baste well with the sauce, and bake, uncovered, for 15 minutes more. Serve with some of the sauce spooned over each piece of chicken.

Serves 4

✳ Chicken and Spaghetti

This recipe is one of our longer ones, but it is well worth the effort.

8 chicken breast halves, skin on
2 cups water
$3/4$ pound fresh mushrooms, sliced
$1/4$ cup margarine ($1/2$ stick), divided
$1/2$ pound spaghetti, noodles broken in half
3 tablespoons all-purpose flour
$1/2$ cup white wine
1 cup heavy cream
Salt
1 pound cooked ham, skin and fat removed, diced into $1/4$-inch cubes
5 ounces slivered almonds ($1/2$ cup)
$3/4$ cup grated Parmesan cheese
Paprika

NOW

In a large saucepan over medium–high heat, combine the chicken breasts with the water. Bring to boil and reduce the heat to low. Simmer the chicken covered, until thoroughly cooked, about 30 minutes. Set aside, reserving both the chicken and the cooking liquid. Remove the chicken from its bones, and rip it into large bite-sized pieces, discarding the skin and the bones. Put the chicken pieces in an airtight container, and set aside. Allow the liquid that the chicken cooked in to cool, skim the fat from the top, and strain. Pour the strained liquid over the chicken, and refrigerate overnight.

Grease a 3-quart baking dish, and set aside. In a medium skillet over medium heat, cook the mushrooms in 1 tablespoon of the margarine, stirring frequently, until softened. Set aside. Cook the spaghetti in plenty of salted boiling water for about 8 minutes. Drain, rinse under cold water, and set aside.

Melt the remaining 3 tablespoons margarine in a medium skillet over medium heat. Slowly add the flour and whisk until smooth. Add 1$^1\!/_2$ cups of the liquid from the chicken, whisking as you do. Reduce the heat to medium-low and cook the sauce, whisking often, until it thickens. Remove the sauce from the heat, add the wine and cream, and season with salt to taste. Mix gently to combine, and set aside.

Drain off and discard any remaining liquid from the chicken. In a large pot, combine the spaghetti, cream sauce, chicken, ham, mushrooms, and almonds, and mix well. Transfer to the prepared baking dish. Top with the Parmesan, and sprinkle with paprika to taste. Cover well and refrigerate for 3 to 12 hours, or freeze for up to 3 months.

LATER

If frozen, allow the casserole to thaw overnight in the refrigerator. Remove it from the refrigerator and let it sit for 1 hour before cooking. Preheat the oven to 350°F. Bake, uncovered, for 45 minutes, until thoroughly hot.

Serves 10 to 12

✳ Party Chicken

A wonderful combination of flavors.

4 large whole chicken breasts, skinned, boned, and split
8 slices bacon
One 4-ounce jar chipped beef
One 10³/₄-ounce can mushroom soup
1 cup sour cream

NOW

Grease a 9 x 13-inch baking dish, and set aside. Wrap each chicken breast half with a slice of bacon. Cover the bottom of the prepared dish with the chipped beef, and arrange the chicken breasts on top. In a small bowl, combine the soup and sour cream, mixing well. Pour the soup mixture over the chicken. Cover well and refrigerate for at least 4 hours or up to 24 hours.

LATER

Preheat the oven to 275°F. Bake, uncovered, for 3 hours.

Serves 8

Swiss Chicken

This is incredibly easy to make—and the Swiss cheese and almonds make a great taste combination.

4 cups cooked chicken, coarsely chopped
2 cups finely chopped celery
2 cups toasted bread cubes
1 cup mayonnaise
1 pinch of pepper
$^{1}/_{2}$ cup milk
$^{1}/_{4}$ cup finely chopped onion
1 teaspoon salt
8 ounces sliced Swiss cheese, cut into thin strips
$^{1}/_{4}$ cup slivered almonds

NOW

Grease a 9 x 13-inch baking dish, and set aside. In a large bowl, combine the chicken, celery, bread cubes, mayonnaise, pepper, milk, onion, salt, and Swiss cheese, and mix well. Spoon into the prepared baking dish, and sprinkle with the almonds. Refrigerate for 3 hours or overnight.

LATER

Preheat the oven to 350°F. Bake the casserole, covered, for 50 minutes, and then uncovered for 10 minutes more, until lightly golden brown. (This dish can also be cooked immediately after making it, in which case it will need only 30 minutes of baking.)

Serves 4 to 6

Poppy Seed Chicken

This is such a delicious and great-looking dish, your guests won't be able to figure out how you made it.

NOW

2 tablespoons margarine

2 pounds boneless chicken breasts, cut into bite-sized pieces

2 cloves garlic, thinly sliced

1 cup sour cream

One 10¾-ounce can cream of chicken soup

¼ cup milk

¼ cup sherry

1 teaspoon dried crumbled oregano

Salt and pepper

LATER

1 cup crushed buttery cracker crumbs

2 tablespoons poppy seeds

2 tablespoons margarine, melted

NOW

Melt the margarine in a large, heavy skillet over medium-high heat. Add the chicken and garlic. Lightly brown the chicken, turning the pieces to brown as much of their surface area as possible. Transfer the chicken to a 2-quart baking dish. In a medium bowl, combine the sour cream, soup, milk, and sherry. Stir in the oregano, and salt and pepper to taste. Pour the sauce over the chicken. Cover and refrigerate for 3 hours or overnight.

LATER

Preheat the oven to 375°F. Top the chicken mixture with the cracker crumbs and poppy seeds. Then drizzle with the melted margarine. Bake the casserole, uncovered, for 30 to 35 minutes, until bubbly.

TIP You can substitute brandy for sherry if you're looking for a different taste. And if you prefer to use no alcohol at all, use $1/2$ cup milk instead.

Serves 4 to 6

Poulet Artichoke

Another elegant dish.

NOW

Two 14-ounce cans artichoke hearts, drained and cut into bite-sized
    pieces
2 whole chicken breasts, cooked and cut into bite-sized pieces
One 4-ounce cans sliced mushrooms, drained
Two 10³/₄-ounce can cream of chicken soup
1 cup mayonnaise
1 teaspoon curry powder
1 tablespoon lemon juice
8 ounces sharp cheddar cheese, grated (2 cups)

4 cups cooked rice

NOW

Grease a 9 x 13-inch baking dish. Spread the artichoke hearts over the bottom of the dish, and cover with the chicken pieces. In a medium bowl, combine the mushrooms, soup, mayonnaise, curry powder, and lemon juice, and mix well. Pour the sauce over the chicken, and sprinkle the cheese on top. Cover the casserole, and refrigerate for 3 hours or up to 2 days.

LATER

Remove the casserole from the refrigerator, and let it sit for 20 to 30 minutes. Preheat the oven to 350°F. Bake the casserole, uncovered, for 30 minutes. Serve over the rice.

Serves 6 to 8

Fiesta Chicken

Tangy and colorful — caramba!

NOW

One 15-ounce can chili (without beans)

1 cup salsa

6 to 8 green onions (scallions), finely chopped

One 4$^1/_4$-ounce can sliced black olives, drained

1 teaspoon salt

$^3/_8$ cup cream cheese (3 ounces), softened

4 whole chicken breasts, cooked and cut into large bite-sized pieces

4 cups grated cheddar-jack cheese (or use cheddar or Monterey Jack cheese or a combination)

LATER

4 cups cooked rice, or 12 ounces crushed tortilla chips

NOW

Lightly grease a 9 x 13-inch baking dish, and set aside. In a large bowl, combine the chili, salsa, green onions, olives, salt, and cream cheese. Add the chicken, and mix well. Pour into the prepared baking dish, and top with the cheese. Cover and refrigerate for 3 hours or up to 2 days.

LATER

Preheat the oven to 350°F. Bake the casserole, uncovered, for 30 to 45 minutes, until thoroughly heated and bubbly. Serve over the rice or crushed tortilla chips.

Serves 6 to 8

Enchiladas de Pollo

These enchiladas can form the centerpiece of a marvelous Mexican dinner. Serve with Mexican Rice (page 216).

NOW

3 tablespoons margarine

1 large onion, finely chopped

$^3/_4$ cup finely chopped celery

One 10-ounce can tomatoes and green chiles

2 whole boneless chicken breasts, cooked and shredded

Two 2$^1/_4$-ounce cans sliced ripe olives, drained

4 cups sour cream

2 tablespoons chicken bouillon granules

Vegetable oil

24 corn tortillas

1 pound Monterey Jack cheese, grated (4 cups)

LATER

$^1/_2$ cup finely chopped green onions (scallions)

NOW

Grease a 9 x 13-inch baking dish and set aside. Melt the margarine in a large skillet over medium heat. Add the onion and celery, and cook, stirring frequently, until they begin to soften. Add the tomatoes and chiles, chicken, and olives, and stir well. Reduce the heat to low, and simmer for 10 minutes. Remove from heat, and set aside.

In a medium saucepan over medium heat, combine the sour cream and bouillon granules and cook, stirring constantly, just until the granules have thoroughly dissolved. Remove from heat, and set aside.

Heat about 1 inch of the oil in a skillet over medium heat, being careful not to overheat it. Carefully dip the tortillas in the oil, one at a time, to soften them, about 10 to 20 seconds each. (Do *not* let them crisp.) Drain the tortillas on paper towels.

Onto each tortilla, spread about 2 tablespoons of the chicken mixture, 1 tablespoon of the sour cream mixture, and 1 tablespoon of the cheese. Roll each tortilla into a cylinder and place it, seam side down, in the prepared baking dish. Top the rolled tortillas with the remaining sour cream sauce and remaining cheese. Cover and refrigerate for 3 hours or up to 2 days.

LATER

Preheat the oven to 350°F. Bake the enchiladas, uncovered, for 35 to 45 minutes, until bubbly. Top with the green onions.

Serves 12

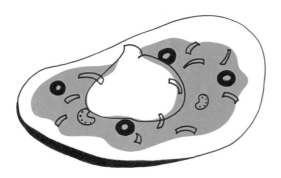

Turkey Tetrazzini

Here's the perfect way to serve leftover turkey.

12 ounces spaghetti or angel-hair pasta, noodles broken in half
One 4-ounce can sliced mushrooms, liquid drained and reserved
1 teaspoon celery salt
1 pinch cayenne pepper
1 teaspoon dried marjoram
One 10^3/$_4$-ounce can cream of chicken or cream of celery soup
One 12-ounce can (1^1/$_2$ cups) evaporated milk
One 2-ounce jar pimientos
^{1}/$_4$ cup butter (^{1}/$_2$ stick)
1 medium yellow onion, finely chopped
2 medium stalks celery, finely sliced
2 cups coarsely chopped cooked turkey
4 ounces cheddar cheese, grated (1 cup)
^{1}/$_4$ cup grated Parmesan cheese

NOW

Grease a 9 x 13-inch baking dish, and set aside. Cook the pasta according to package directions until al dente, drain, and set aside. In a medium bowl, combine the reserved mushroom liquid, celery salt, cayenne pepper, marjoram, soup, evaporated milk, and pimientos, and set aside.

Melt the butter in a large skillet over medium–high heat. Add the onion, celery, and mushrooms. Cook, stirring frequently, until the onion and celery have softened. Stir in the evaporated milk mixture, and continue cooking, stirring frequently, until the sauce begins to thicken, about 3 to 5 minutes.

MAKE IT NOW, BAKE IT LATER!

Stir the soup mixture into the onion and celery, and cook until the sauce is smooth and thick. Add the turkey, pour the sauce over the pasta, and mix thoroughly. Transfer to the prepared baking dish, and top with the cheeses. Cover and refrigerate for 2 hours or overnight.

LATER

Preheat the oven to 350°F. Bake the tetrazzini, uncovered, for 30 to 45 minutes, until bubbly.

TIP Sometimes, instead of leftover turkey, we'll buy a ½-inch to 1-inch slice of very good turkey from the deli counter and dice it for this dish. No one can tell the difference! Also, this recipe can be made with chicken. And if you've made it the day before and you think it looks too dry, drizzle the tetrazzini with some chicken broth before baking.

Serves 8 to 10

Pork Chops Milano

Amid the hustle and bustle of Milan, the booming industrial city and fashion capital of Italy, people still know how to enjoy a good chop!

NOW

6 pork loin chops

2 tablespoons all-purpose flour

2 teaspoons salt, divided

$^3/_4$ teaspoon pepper, divided

$^1/_2$ teaspoon paprika

$^1/_4$ teaspoon nutmeg

2 tablespoons vegetable oil

2 tablespoons butter

$^1/_2$ cup finely chopped onion

$^1/_2$ cup finely chopped green bell pepper

One 28-ounce can crushed tomatoes

One 15-ounce can tomato sauce

$^1/_2$ cup dry red wine

2 tablespoons tomato paste

2 cloves garlic, crushed

$^1/_2$ teaspoon sugar

1 tablespoon dried (crumbled) oregano

1 tablespoon dried basil

$^1/_2$ teaspoon dried thyme

LATER

12 ounces macaroni

$^1/_4$ cup grated Parmesan cheese, plus more for serving

NOW

Grease a 9 x 13-inch baking dish, and set aside. Trim excess fat off the pork chops. In a large, resealable plastic bag, combine the flour, 1 teaspoon of salt, 1/2 teaspoon of pepper, paprika, and nutmeg. Put the pork chops in the bag and shake to coat. Shake off excess flour, and set aside.

In a large skillet over medium-high heat, heat the oil and butter. Brown the coated chops quickly on both sides. Place them in the prepared baking dish, and set aside.

In the same skillet over medium-high heat, cook the onion and bell pepper until tender, about 5 minutes. Add the crushed tomatoes, tomato sauce, wine, tomato paste, garlic, remaining 1 teaspoon salt, sugar, oregano, basil, thyme, and the remaining 1/4 teaspoon pepper. Bring to a boil, and reduce the heat to low. Simmer, stirring occasionally, for about 20 minutes. Pour this sauce over the chops, and allow it to cool. Cover and refrigerate for 3 hours or up to 2 days.

LATER

Remove the chops from the refrigerator, and let them sit for 20 to 30 minutes. Preheat the oven to 325°F. Bake, covered, for 2 hours. Cook the macaroni according the package directions. Drain and toss in a large bowl with the cheese. Remove the pork chops from the oven, and place them on top of the macaroni. Top with the tomato sauce that cooked with the chops. Serve with additional Parmesan cheese on the side.

TIP If you're in a hurry, make the entire dish in your skillet. Once you have made the sauce, put the pork chops back in the sauce. Reduce the heat to medium and cook, covered, for 25 to 30 minutes, or until tender.

Serves 6

✳ Saucy Pork Chops

This approach to cooking pork chops ensures that they'll be a sure-fire hit.

4 center-cut loin pork chops, 1¹/₂ inches thick
¹/₂ cup ketchup
1¹/₂ teaspoons salt
¹/₂ teaspoon chili powder
1 cup water
1¹/₂ teaspoons dry mustard
1 tablespoon dark brown sugar
1 lemon, sliced
1 small yellow onion, sliced

NOW

Grease a 9 x 9-inch baking dish. Place the chops in the dish in one layer. In a medium bowl, combine the ketchup, salt, chili powder, water, dry mustard, and brown sugar, and mix well. Pour the sauce over the chops. Arrange one slice of lemon and one slice of onion on top of each chop. Cover and refrigerate for up to 24 hours.

LATER

Preheat the oven to 325°F. Bake the pork chops, covered, for 2 hours. Remove the cover and baste well with the sauce. Continue baking, uncovered, for 30 minutes more. Spoon the sauce over the chops again before serving.

Serves 4

MAKE IT NOW, BAKE IT LATER!

Stew Brazil

This delicious stew evokes the exotic flavors of this mammoth, tropical country and its abundance of unique dishes.

NOW
1/4 cup peanut oil
1 pound Italian sausage, cut into bite-sized pieces
2 large pork chops, cut into bite-sized pieces
1 pound round steak, cut into bite-sized pieces
1/2 cup finely chopped yellow onion
2 cloves garlic, crushed
1 tablespoon dark brown sugar
1 1/2 teaspoons salt
1/2 teaspoon turmeric
1/4 teaspoon cayenne pepper
1/4 teaspoon dried (crumbled) oregano
1 pinch of saffron
1 large green bell pepper, cut into thin strips
1 tablespoon vinegar
1/2 cup water

LATER
One 2-ounce jar diced pimientos
4 cups hot cooked rice
1/2 cup chopped peanuts

NOW

Heat the oil in a large pot over medium-high heat. Brown the sausage pieces, discarding all but about 1/4 cup excess fat to facilitate browning. Remove the sausage from the pot and drain on paper towels. Add the pork chop pieces to the pot, brown them, and drain them on paper towels. Then, in the same pot, brown the steak pieces, and drain them on paper towels.

Put the onion and garlic in the pot, and cook them until golden. Return the browned meats to the pot. Add the brown sugar, salt, turmeric, cayenne, oregano, saffron, bell pepper, vinegar, and water, and mix well. Reduce the heat to low, cover, and simmer for 45 minutes. Remove the stew from heat, and allow it to cool. Refrigerate overnight or up to 3 days.

LATER

Reheat the stew over medium heat, stirring frequently. When hot, add the pimientos. Spoon the stew over a bed of cooked rice, and sprinkle the peanuts on top.

Serves 6

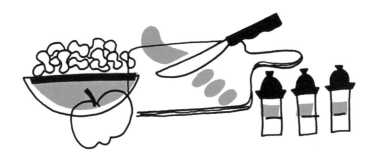

Baby Back Ribs

These ribs are so delicious, you'll never seem to have enough.

6 pounds pork baby back ribs, cut into serving-sized pieces
$1^1/_2$ cups ketchup
$^3/_4$ cup firmly packed dark brown sugar
$^1/_2$ cup white distilled vinegar
$^1/_2$ cup honey
$^1/_3$ cup soy sauce
$1^1/_2$ teaspoons ginger
1 teaspoon salt
$^3/_4$ teaspoon dry mustard
$^1/_2$ teaspoon garlic powder
$^1/_4$ teaspoon pepper

NOW

Preheat the oven to 350°F. Arrange the ribs on roasting racks in baking pans, meaty side up. Cover with aluminum foil, and bake for $1^1/_4$ hours, until tender. Remove the ribs from the oven, and allow them to cool.

In a medium bowl, combine the remaining ingredients, and mix well. Coat the ribs with the sauce, and refrigerate in an airtight container for 3 hours or up to 2 days in the refrigerator.

LATER

Preheat the oven to 350°F. Bake the ribs for 35 minutes. (You can also grill the ribs.)

Serves 8

Potluck Ham Casserole

Some of the dishes served at those old-fashioned potluck dinners were actually pretty good! Here's a prime example.

One 10³/₄-ounce can cream of celery soup
1¹/₂ cups mayonnaise
¹/₂ teaspoon pepper
1¹/₂ tablespoons lemon juice
1 tablespoon dry mustard
3 cups cooked rice
3 cups finely cubed ham
3 cups grated cheddar cheese, divided
One 8-ounce can water chestnuts, finely diced
1¹/₂ cups finely chopped celery
1 medium yellow onion, finely chopped
¹/₄ cup grated Parmesan cheese
One 4¹/₄-ounce can sliced ripe olives
One 2-ounce jar pimientos
3 cups crushed cornflakes cereal
¹/₄ cup butter (¹/₂ stick), melted

NOW

Grease a 9 x 13-inch baking dish, and set aside. In a medium bowl, combine the soup, mayonnaise, pepper, lemon juice, and dry mustard, and mix well. In a large bowl, combine the rice, ham, cheddar, water chestnuts, celery, onion, cheese, olives, and pimientos, and mix well. Add the soup mixture, and stir thoroughly. Transfer to the prepared baking dish, and set aside. In a medium bowl, combine the cornflakes and butter and spread evenly over the top of the casserole. Cover and refrigerate overnight or up to 2 days.

LATER

Preheat the oven to 350°F. Bake the casserole, uncovered, for 45 minutes, until bubbly.

Serves 10 to 12

Barbecued Butterflied Lamb

This was a secret recipe for many years, but we've now decided to share it! Lamb prepared this way has a fabulous taste that you will love.

1 cup dry red wine
$^{1}/_{2}$ cup olive oil
$^{1}/_{3}$ cup chili sauce
2 tablespoons finely chopped parsley
2 tablespoons finely chopped chives or green onion (scallion) tops
$^{1}/_{2}$ teaspoon Worcestershire sauce
$^{1}/_{4}$ teaspoon freshly ground black pepper
$^{1}/_{4}$ teaspoon dried marjoram
$^{1}/_{4}$ teaspoon dried rosemary
$^{1}/_{4}$ teaspoon dried thyme
2 cloves garlic, mashed with 1 teaspoon salt
1 leg of lamb (about 5 to 6 pounds), pounded to an even 2-inch thickness,
   not flat like a pancake

NOW

In an airtight container large enough to accommodate the lamb, combine the wine, oil, chili sauce, parsley, chives, Worcestershire sauce, pepper, marjoram, rosemary, thyme, and garlic, and mix well. Add the lamb, close the container, and shake well to coat. (The marinade should almost cover the lamb.) Refrigerate overnight or up to 2 days. Periodically, shake the container to keep the lamb moist.

LATER

Remove the lamb from the refrigerator, and let it sit for up to 1 hour to come to room temperature before grilling.

Preheat a barbecue or grill to medium-high heat (as for a steak), and grill the lamb for about 20 minutes on each side. (The lamb should be slightly pink in the center. If you prefer it well done, cook it longer.) Remove the lamb from heat, cover it with aluminum foil, and let it sit for 15 minutes before carving. Slice the lamb across the grain into $\frac{1}{2}$-inch slices.

TIP You can reuse the marinade during grilling or as a serving sauce: After marinating the lamb, transfer the liquid to a medium saucepan over medium-high heat. Bring it to a boil and let it boil vigorously for at least 2 minutes. Brush the marinade on the lamb as it grills, or serve it on the side.

Serves 6

✳ Lamb Shanks Deluxe

This wonderful dish is very fragrant while it bakes, and the gravy is delicious over mashed potatoes.

NOW

4 to 5 pounds meaty lamb shanks

$^1/_2$ lemon

$^1/_4$ teaspoon garlic powder

1 cup all-purpose flour

2 teaspoons salt

$^1/_2$ teaspoon pepper

$^1/_2$ cup salad oil

One $10^3/_4$-ounce can condensed beef consommé ($1^1/_3$ cups)

1 cup water

$^1/_2$ cup dry vermouth

1 medium yellow onion, finely chopped

LATER

4 medium carrots, peeled and coarsely chopped

4 medium stalks celery, coarsely chopped

NOW

Rub the lamb with the lemon, and sprinkle it with the garlic powder. Let it sit for 10 minutes. In a small paper bag or large resealable plastic bag, combine the flour, salt, and pepper. Shake the shanks in the bag, one at a time, to coat them with the flour. Set the flour mixture aside.

Heat the oil in a large skillet over medium-high heat. Brown the floured shanks in the hot oil, turning them to brown all sides. Remove the meat from the pan, and set it aside. Add 4 tablespoons of the reserved flour to the pan drippings and, using a whisk, stir and brown the flour. Add the consommé, water, and vermouth, and cook, whisking frequently, until the gravy is slightly thickened. Add the onion, mix well, and remove from heat. Set aside.

Place the shanks in a baking dish large enough to accommodate them in one layer. Pour the gravy over them. Cover well and refrigerate for up to 24 hours.

LATER

Preheat the oven to 350°F. Bake the shanks, uncovered, for 1½ hours. Turn the shanks, add the carrots and celery, and bake for 1 hour more.

Serves 4

✳ Shrimp and Cheese Casserole

This is the very first recipe from the first Make It Now, Bake It Later! *cookbook. It was one of Mother's favorites! In fact, this is virtually the only dish that Scott ever served to guests as a bachelor. Now, after thirty years of marriage, it is still one of the most requested.*

> 6 slices white bread
> 1½ pounds shrimp, cooked, cleaned, and peeled
> ½ pound American cheese slices, cut into small pieces
> ½ cup butter (1 stick), melted
> 3 eggs, lightly beaten

$^1/_2$ teaspoon dry mustard
Salt and white pepper
2 cups milk

NOW

Grease a 2-quart baking dish, and set aside. Tear the bread into pieces about the size of a quarter. Arrange the shrimp, bread, and cheese in several layers in the prepared dish. Pour the melted butter evenly over the top, and set aside. In a medium bowl, combine the eggs and the mustard, and mix well. Season with salt and white pepper. Add the milk, mix together, and pour this mixture over the casserole. Cover and refrigerate for at least 3 hours or preferably overnight.

LATER

Preheat the oven to 350°F. Bake the casserole, covered, for 1 hour, until the cheese is bubbly.

TIP Add a green salad and crusty French bread to make a perfect meal—you will get lots of raves!

Serves 4

Fantastic Shrimp

*Our wonderful friend, Rachel, an impeccable hostess, dazzles her guests
with this great recipe.*

NOW

$^1/_2$ cup butter or margarine (1 stick), divided

8 ounces fresh mushrooms, sliced, or one 16-ounce can sliced
    mushrooms, liquid drained and reserved

$^1/_3$ cup sherry

Milk, as needed

5 tablespoons all-purpose flour

$^1/_4$ cup finely chopped yellow onion

1 teaspoon dried basil

1 teaspoon dried parsley

$^1/_8$ teaspoon cayenne pepper

$^1/_2$ teaspoon curry powder

1 dash of hot pepper sauce

1 to 2 teaspoons salt

$^1/_2$ cup grated Parmesan cheese

2 pounds medium shrimp, peeled, boiled, and drained

8 ounces Monterey Jack cheese, grated (2 cups)

2 tablespoons butter, cut into small pieces

1 teaspoon garlic powder

LATER

Paprika

6 cups hot cooked rice

NOW

Spray a 9 x 13-inch baking dish with vegetable cooking spray, and set aside.

In a large skillet over medium-high heat, melt 2 tablespoons of the butter. Add the mushrooms and cook, stirring frequently, until they have softened. Drain the mushrooms, reserving the mushroom liquid. Combine the sherry with the mushroom liquid and enough milk to make 2 cups liquid, and set aside.

In a large skillet over medium heat, melt the remaining 6 tablespoons butter. Stir in the flour, mixing well. Add the sherry-mushroom liquid. Continue cooking, stirring constantly, until the sauce thickens. Reduce the heat to low, and add the onion, basil, parsley, cayenne pepper, curry powder, hot pepper sauce, salt, and Parmesan. Mix well, and cook the sauce for 2 minutes more. Fold in the shrimp and reserved mushrooms, and remove from heat.

Pour the shrimp mixture into the prepared baking dish. Top with the Monterey Jack cheese, dot with the pieces of butter, and sprinkle with the garlic powder. Cover and refrigerate overnight or preferably a day or two. (Do not freeze.)

LATER

Preheat the oven to 350°F. Sprinkle the top of the casserole with paprika and bake, uncovered, for 30 to 40 minutes, until bubbly. Transfer to a preheated broiler and allow the casserole to brown lightly, about 1 to 2 minutes, watching carefully to make sure it does not burn. Let it cool for 10 to 15 minutes before serving over rice.

TIP You can also serve this shrimp dish in pastry shells, which makes a lovely presentation.

Serves 8 to 12

Seaside Seafood

This is a wonderful dish for a special party.

1 cup breadcrumbs
9 tablespoons butter (1 stick plus 1 tablespoon), melted and divided
1 cup finely chopped yellow onion
1 cup finely chopped celery
1 large green bell pepper, finely chopped
1 package Uncle Ben's long grain and wild rice, prepared according to the
    package directions (about 3 cups cooked rice)
2 pounds small shrimp, cooked and peeled
1 pound crabmeat (fresh or canned)
Three $10^3/_4$-ounce cans cream of celery soup
One 8-ounce can sliced mushrooms, drained
$^1/_2$ cup slivered almonds
One 4-ounce jar diced pimientos

NOW

Grease a 4-quart baking dish (or two 2-quart baking dishes), and set aside.
In a small bowl, combine the breadcrumbs with 1 tablespoon of the melted
butter. Mix well and set aside.

In a large saucepan over medium heat, combine the onion, celery, and the
remaining $^1/_2$ cup melted butter. Cook, stirring frequently, until the onion
and celery are tender. Remove the vegetables from the heat, and add the
bell pepper, cooked rice, shrimp, crabmeat, soup, mushrooms, almonds,
and pimientos. Stir gently to combine.

Spoon into the prepared baking dish or dishes. Top with the breadcrumb
mixture. Cover and refrigerate overnight, or freeze for up to 1 month

LATER

If frozen, allow the casserole to thaw overnight in the refrigerator. Remove from the refrigerator, and let it sit for 20 to 30 minutes. Preheat the oven to 350°F. Bake the casserole for 30 to 45 minutes, until bubbly.

Serves 12 to 15

Neptune's Delight

A seafood lover's favorite.

1 cup crabmeat (fresh or canned)
1 cup small cooked and peeled shrimp
1 cup finely chopped celery
$1/2$ cup finely chopped yellow onion
$1/2$ cup finely chopped green bell pepper
$1/4$ cup finely chopped red bell pepper
One 8-ounce can sliced water chestnuts
1 cup mayonnaise
2 cups seasoned croutons
1 tablespoon Worcestershire sauce

NOW

Grease a 9 x 9-inch baking dish, and set aside. In a large bowl, gently combine all the ingredients, and transfer to the prepared baking dish. Cover and refrigerate overnight.

LATER

Preheat the oven to 350°F. Bake the casserole, uncovered, for 30 minutes, until bubbly.

Serves 4 to 6

✳ Marinade for Fish

This marinade makes any fish taste great!

NOW
1 clove garlic, finely minced
$^1\!/_2$ cup soy sauce
$^1\!/_2$ cup red wine
1 tablespoon lemon juice

LATER
$^1\!/_4$ cup finely chopped green onions (scallions)

NOW

In a medium bowl, combine the garlic, soy sauce, wine, and lemon juice, and mix well. Use this sauce to marinate fish, covered, in the refrigerator for 3 hours, turning once. (If the fish is whole or the fillets are thick, make two or three gashes in the flesh before marinating.)

If baking, sprinkle the fish with green onions beforehand. If broiling or grilling, sprinkle the green onions on after cooking.

Makes enough marinade for 3 to 4 pounds firm-fleshed fish

Sunday Strata

This dish is so tasty, we could eat it morning, noon, and night, every day of the week! It's our signature Sunday brunch dish.

12 slices white bread, crusts removed
3 tablespoons butter or margarine, softened
$^1/_2$ cup butter or margarine (1 stick)
$^1/_2$ pound fresh mushrooms, sliced; or one 8-ounce can sliced mushrooms, drained
1 large yellow onion, thinly sliced
Salt and pepper
2 pounds mild Italian sausage meat, cooked and crumbled
1 pound cheddar cheese, grated (4 cups)
5 eggs
$2^1/_2$ cups milk
3 teaspoons Dijon mustard
1 teaspoon dry mustard
1 teaspoon ground nutmeg
1 teaspoon salt
$^1/_4$ teaspoon pepper

NOW

Lightly grease a 9 x 13-inch baking dish, and set aside. Butter the bread with the 3 tablespoons softened butter, and fit 6 of the slices, butter side up, in the prepared baking dish. Set the other 6 slices aside. In a large skillet over medium heat, melt the $\frac{1}{2}$ cup butter, and cook the mushrooms and onion until tender. Season with salt and pepper to taste. Remove from heat, add the sausage meat, and mix well.

On top of the bread in the dish, layer one-half of the sausage mixture and one-half of the cheese. Add a second layer of bread, then the rest of the sausage mixture, and end with the cheese. In a medium bowl, combine the eggs, milk, Dijon mustard, dry mustard, nutmeg, salt, and pepper, and mix well. Pour the egg mixture over the casserole. Cover and refrigerate overnight.

LATER

Preheat the oven to 350°F. Bake the casserole, uncovered, for 45 to 60 minutes, until bubbly. Serve immediately.

Serves 8 to 10

Tucson Strata

This delicious egg dish can be the centerpiece of a brunch or a side dish for a more elaborate meal.

NOW
3 tablespoons butter, softened
6 slices bread, crusts removed
4 cups grated cheddar-jack cheese (or use cheddar or Monterey Jack cheese, or a combination)
Two 4-ounce cans diced green chiles
6 eggs
2 cups milk
1 teaspoon salt
2 teaspoons paprika
1 teaspoon dried (crumbled) oregano
$1/2$ teaspoon garlic powder
$1/4$ teaspoon dry mustard

LATER
Salsa, for serving

NOW

Spread the butter on one side of each slice of bread. Arrange the slices, butter side down, in a 9 x 13-inch baking dish. Sprinkle the cheese evenly over bread. Layer the chiles evenly on top.

In a medium bowl, beat the eggs, milk, salt, paprika, oregano, garlic powder, and dry mustard with a whisk until well blended. Pour the egg mixture over the casserole. Cover and refrigerate overnight, or for at least 4 hours.

LATER
Preheat the oven to 325°F. Bake the casserole, uncovered, for about 50 minutes, until the top is lightly browned. Warm the salsa in a small saucepan over medium heat for about 5 minutes. Let the casserole stand for 10 minutes before serving with the warmed salsa on the side.

Serves 8 to 10

New Orleans French Toast

Here's a scrumptious, rich morning meal with no early-morning work!

NOW
1/2 cup unsalted butter (1 stick)
1 cup firmly packed dark brown sugar
2 tablespoons light corn syrup
1 loaf challah or French bread
5 eggs
1 1/2 cups half-and-half
1 tablespoon Grand Marnier, optional
1 tablespoon vanilla (or 2 tablespoons if not using the Grand Marnier)
1/4 teaspoon salt

LATER
Maple syrup, for serving

NOW

Lightly grease a 9 x 13-inch baking dish, and set aside. Melt the butter in a small heavy saucepan over medium heat. Add the brown sugar and corn syrup. Cook, stirring frequently, until the mixture is smooth. Pour the sugar mixture into the prepared dish, and set aside.

Make six to eight 1-inch-thick slices from the center of the loaf of bread. Place the slices in one layer on top of the sugar mixture, squeezing them together, if necessary, to make them fit. Set aside.

In a medium bowl whisk together the eggs, half-and-half, Grand Marnier, if using, vanilla, and salt. Pour this mixture evenly over the bread in the baking dish. Cover and refrigerate, for at least 8 hours or up to 1 day.

LATER

Remove the French toast from the refrigerator, and let it sit for 20 to 30 minutes. Preheat the oven to 350°F. Bake, uncovered, until the bread has puffed and the edges are golden, 35 to 40 minutes. Serve the hot French toast immediately with syrup on the side.

TIP Serve this with fresh fruit and you have a terrific breakfast for guests.

Serves 6 to 8

Adobe Huevos!

A hearty meal with a great South-of-the-Border flavor.

1 pound sausage meat

6 eggs

1 cup sour cream

3 green onions (scallions), finely chopped

1 teaspoon ground cumin

$^1/_4$ teaspoon hot pepper sauce

$^1/_2$ teaspoon salt

$^1/_4$ teaspoon pepper

4 cups grated cheddar-jack cheese (or use cheddar or Monterey Jack
    cheese, or a combination), divided

One 4-ounce can green chiles, chopped and drained

1 cup thick and chunky salsa

$^1/_2$ teaspoon salt

NOW

Preheat the oven to 350°F. Lightly grease a 9 x 13-inch baking dish, and set aside. In a large skillet on medium-high heat, cook the sausage thoroughly, crumbling it as it cooks. Remove from heat, pour off and discard the fat, and transfer the sausage bits to paper towels to drain.

In a medium bowl, combine the eggs and sour cream, and beat well with a whisk. Add the green onions, cumin, hot pepper sauce, salt, and pepper, and mix well. Pour the egg mixture into the prepared baking dish, and bake for 5 minutes. Stir the mixture, moving the more cooked outer edges into the center, and bake for 5 minutes more. Stir the mixture and bake again (for a total baking time of 15 minutes).

Evenly spread a layer of 2 cups of cheese over the egg mixture. Spread chiles over the cheese, and sausage over the chiles. Follow with the salsa and then the remaining 2 cups cheese. Cover and refrigerate overnight.

LATER

Preheat the oven to 325°F. Bake the casserole, uncovered, for 35 to 45 minutes, until the cheese melts and the edges bubble.

Serves 8 to 10

Orange Blintz Soufflé

This is a wonderful breakfast dish that is light, intriguing, and delectable.

NOW
¹/₄ cup butter (¹/₂ stick), softened
¹/₃ cup sugar
6 whole eggs plus 2 egg yolks
1¹/₂ cups sour cream
¹/₂ cup freshly squeezed orange juice
1 cup all-purpose flour
2 teaspoons baking powder
1 cup cream cheese (8 ounces)
2 cups small-curd cottage cheese
2 tablespoons sugar
1 teaspoon vanilla
Zest of 1 orange

Optional toppings

Sour cream

Maple syrup

Jam (such as orange marmalade)

NOW

Grease a 9 x 13-inch baking dish, and set aside. In a blender or food processor, combine the butter, sugar, whole eggs, sour cream, orange juice, flour, and baking powder. Pulse until just blended. Pour half the batter into the prepared baking dish. Set the remaining batter aside.

In blender or food processor, combine the cream cheese, cottage cheese, egg yolks, sugar, and vanilla. Pulse until well mixed, adding the orange zest at the end. Drop by heaping tablespoons over the batter in the baking dish to cover the batter completely. With the edge of a knife, gently smooth the top. Pour the remaining batter on top. Cover and refrigerate for 3 hours or overnight.

LATER

Remove the soufflé from the refrigerator, and let it sit for 20 to 30 minutes. Preheat the oven to 350°F. Bake the soufflé, uncovered, for 50 to 60 minutes, until puffed and golden. Serve immediately with sour cream, syrup, or jam.

Serves 6 to 8

Breads and Side Dishes

Breads are wonderful as the main course at a morning coffee, or a rich and wholesome adjunct to your feature attraction at lunch or dinner. What's more enticing to your family and friends than the fragrant smell of fresh muffins or bread coming out of the oven? The smell of baking bread evokes powerful and wonderful memories of family, childhood, and great home entertaining. We've decided to group breads with side dishes because they offer a very distinct addition to your dinner, while rarely overshadowing the main course.

The common criteria for selecting side dishes are color (you want the dish to look good with the main course), a contrast in textures (you want to pair crunchy with soft or sweet with sour), or a belief that the featured vegetable is especially good for you and your family. These are all excellent points, but we tend to focus on one thing—side dishes that taste great! Mushrooms and Rice (page 212) and Cheesy Broccoli (page 236) are a couple of our family's favorites, but you'll find that your family and guests are certain to have their own among these sides. Some of them will be as big a hit as the main course.

Many people think of side dishes as secondary to the feature attraction. In many presentations, of course, that is true. We'd like to admit, though, that the most memorable item for us at potluck dinners, church socials, and the many luncheons we've attended is often a truly great side dish. Since side dishes are generally undervalued, when you have a great one, you remember it. So enjoy our breads and sides—your family may decide one of these recipes should be a "regular."

Friendship Bran Muffins

This handy batter keeps for a couple of weeks in the refrigerator and will provide delicious muffins for family and friends at the drop of a hat.

One 15-ounce box raisin bran cereal
5 cups all-purpose flour
5 teaspoons baking soda
2 teaspoons salt
2¾ cups sugar
4 eggs, lightly beaten
1 cup shortening
1 quart buttermilk

NOW

In a large bowl, combine the cereal, flour, baking soda, salt, and sugar, and mix well. In a medium bowl, combine the eggs, shortening, and buttermilk, and mix well. Stir the egg mixture into the cereal mixture, and mix well. Transfer the batter to an airtight container, and refrigerate for up to 2 weeks.

LATER

Preheat the oven to 400°F. Grease the muffin tins (for 60 muffins), and fill them two-thirds full with the batter. Bake for 15 minutes, or until lightly browned and a toothpick inserted into the center comes out clean.

Makes 5 dozen muffins

Sweet Potato Muffins

These muffins are a wonderful addition to holiday meals, especially Thanksgiving.

1$^1/_2$ cups all-purpose flour
2 teaspoons baking powder
$^1/_4$ teaspoon nutmeg
$^1/_4$ teaspoon salt
1$^1/_2$ teaspoons cinnamon, divided
1$^1/_4$ cups plus 2 tablespoons sugar, divided
1$^1/_4$ cups cooked and mashed sweet potatoes or yams (canned or fresh)
$^1/_2$ cup butter (1 stick), softened
2 eggs
1 cup milk
$^1/_2$ cup raisins
$^1/_4$ cup chopped pecans

NOW

Preheat the oven to 400°F. Generously grease the muffin tins (for 24 muffins), and set aside. In a medium bowl, combine the flour, baking powder, nutmeg, salt, and 1 teaspoon of the cinnamon, and mix well. In a large bowl, combine 1$^1/_4$ cups of the sugar, the sweet potatoes, and butter, and beat with an electric mixer until smooth. Add the eggs and mix well. Alternately add small amounts of the flour mixture and the milk to the sweet potato mixture, stirring just to blend after each addition. Do not overmix. Fold in the raisins and pecans. Spoon the mixture into the prepared muffin cups.

In a small bowl, combine the remaining 2 tablespoons sugar and $^1/_2$ teaspoon cinnamon, and sprinkle the cinnamon-sugar over the muffins.

Bake for 25 to 30 minutes, until lightly browned and a toothpick inserted into the center comes out clean. Allow the muffins to cool thoroughly, transfer them to an airtight container, and freeze for up to 3 months.

LATER

Remove the muffins from the freezer, and allow them to sit at room temperature for 2 hours.

To reheat the muffins in the microwave, put them in a single layer in a resealable plastic bag, but do not seal the bag. Microwave the muffins for 45 seconds to I minute, until thoroughly warmed.

To reheat the muffins in the oven, preheat the oven to 400°F. Wrap the thawed muffins in aluminum foil, and bake them for 15 minutes until thoroughly warmed.

Serve warm.

Makes 24 muffins

Mini Blintzes

These make mornings special. Bet you can't have just one!

NOW

2 large loaves sliced white bread (cheap bread is fine here)

2 teaspoons cinnamon

1 cup sugar, divided

2 cups cream cheese (16 ounces), softened

2 egg yolks

1/2 cup butter (1 stick), melted

LATER

2 cups sour cream

NOW

Remove the crusts and roll each slice of bread flat with a rolling pin. On a dinner plate, combine the cinnamon and 1/2 cup of the sugar, and set aside. In a medium bowl, combine the cream cheese, egg yolks, and the remaining 1/2 cup sugar, and beat with an electric mixer until creamy. Spread the cream cheese mixture on one side of each of the flattened bread slices and roll the bread up like little jelly rolls. Roll each blintz in the melted butter, then in the cinnamon-sugar mixture. Cut each blintz in half, arrange the pieces on a baking sheet, and freeze them, uncovered. Once frozen, transfer the blintzes to freezer bags and return them to the freezer for up to 3 months.

LATER

Preheat the oven to 400°F. Lightly spray a baking sheet with vegetable cooking spray, and place the frozen blintzes on it. Bake for 15 to 20 minutes, until crisp. Serve with sour cream, for dipping.

→ TIP This is another recipe that's great to have on hand in the freezer for an impromptu brunch or coffee.

Makes about 60 blintzes

Herb Cheese Bread

Try this delicious bread with Classic Spinach Salad (page 85) for lunch or with any barbecue.

1 cup butter (2 sticks), melted
1 tablespoon dried parsley
1 tablespoon dried minced onion
2 teaspoons poppy seeds
1 small clove garlic, minced, optional
One 8-ounce block cheddar-jack cheese (or use cheddar or Monterey Jack cheese, or a combination)
1 round loaf sourdough or French bread

NOW

Melt the butter in a small saucepan over medium heat. Add the parsley, onion, poppy seeds, and garlic, and mix well. Remove from heat and set aside. Cut the cheese into $\frac{1}{4}$-inch slices and set aside.

Slice the bread into roughly $1\frac{1}{2}$-inch squares, but do not cut through the bottom crust! (Beginning at the top crust, cut the loaf at $1\frac{1}{2}$-inch intervals, then turn the loaf 90 degrees and repeat to make the squares.) Gently spread the bread squares apart, and drizzle the butter mixture into the cuts, making sure to distribute it throughout the loaf. Insert the cheese slices into the cuts, and wrap the loaf in aluminum foil. Refrigerate for 3 hours or up to 3 days.

LATER

Remove the loaf from the refrigerator, and let it sit, still wrapped in foil, for at least 1 hour. Preheat the oven to 350°F. Place the foil-wrapped loaf on a baking sheet, and bake for 20 minutes. Open the foil to expose the top of the loaf, and bake for 10 minutes more, until lightly browned. Serve hot.

TIP You can use any kind of cheese you want. Try Monterey Jack for a mild taste, but if you like spicier flavors, use Pepper Jack.

Serves 8 to 10

Fancy French Bread

You won't have a slice left!

$^1/_2$ cup butter (1 stick), softened
3 green onions (scallions), finely chopped
1 clove garlic, minced
1 teaspoon dried crumbled oregano
One 4$^1/_4$-ounce can chopped ripe olives, drained well
$^3/_4$ cup grated Parmesan cheese
1 large loaf French or Italian bread, split in half lengthwise

NOW

In a medium bowl, combine the butter, green onions, garlic, oregano, olives, and Parmesan, and mix well. Spread the seasoned butter on the cut sides of the bread. Transfer the halves, butter side up, to a baking sheet, cover, and refrigerate for 3 hours or overnight.

LATER

Preheat the oven to 400°F. Bake the bread, uncovered, for 10 to 15 minutes, until golden brown. Slice into serving pieces, and serve warm.

Serves 6 to 8

✳ Filled French Rolls

These rolls are fun to make and fun to eat, since each person gets his or her own little loaf. They're great for a barbecue!

1/2 cup margarine (1 stick), softened
1/2 cup freshly grated Parmesan cheese
2 tablespoons vegetable oil
1/2 cup finely chopped parsley
1 clove garlic, minced
1/2 teaspoon dried basil
Salt
Eight 6-inch French rolls

NOW

In a medium bowl, combine the margarine, Parmesan, oil, parsley, garlic, and basil. Mix well, and season with salt to taste. From top to bottom, cut each roll into four sections, without cutting through the bottom crust. Spread the butter mixture between each slice, and wrap each roll individually in aluminum foil. Refrigerate for up to 3 days, or freeze for up to 3 months.

LATER

If frozen, allow the rolls to thaw in the refrigerator overnight, or simply bake for 10 minutes longer than described below. Preheat the oven to 375°F. Bake the rolls in the foil for 20 minutes. Serve the rolls in the foil to help keep them warm.

Makes 8 rolls

Orange Rolls

In our house, it's just not a holiday without Grandmother's rolls.

NOW
2 envelopes (4$^1/_2$ teaspoons) active dry yeast, or 3 envelopes if you plan
    to freeze the rolls before cooking (see the TIP on the next page)
$^1/_2$ cup plus 1 pinch sugar, divided
1$^1/_4$ cups warm water (at temperature suggested on the yeast package),
    divided
$^1/_2$ cup butter (1 stick), softened
3 eggs, lightly beaten
4$^1/_2$ cups all-purpose flour
2 teaspoons salt

LATER
Grated zest of 1 large orange
$^1/_2$ cup butter (1 stick), softened
$^1/_2$ cup sugar

NOW
In a large bowl, combine the yeast, 1 pinch of the sugar, and $^1/_2$ cup of the
warm water. Allow the mixture to sit until bubbles form, about 10 minutes.
Add the remaining $^1/_2$ cup sugar, the butter, and eggs, and mix well.
Alternately stir in small amounts of the flour and the remaining $^3/_4$ warm
cup water, mixing well after each addition. Mix in the salt. (This dough is
very soft and can be stirred with a wooden spoon.)

Cover the bowl with a clean dish towel, and let the dough sit in a warm,
draft-free location until it has doubled in volume, about 1 hour. Punch
down the dough. Cover tightly, and refrigerate for up to 3 days.

LATER

Generously grease the muffin tins (for 30 rolls), and set aside. In a small bowl, combine the orange zest, butter, and sugar, and mix them into a paste. Place one-half of the dough on a well-floured surface. Roll it into a large rectangle, as thin as possible, about ⅛- to ¼-inch thick. Spread the rectangle with one-half of the orange butter mixture. Starting with a long edge, roll the rectangle into a tight cylinder, pinching the seam with your fingers to seal it. Cut the resulting cylinder into 1-inch slices, and place them in the prepared muffin tins, cut side up.

Repeat with the remaining dough. (If you want to freeze the dough at this point, see the TIP below.) Cover the muffin tins with clean dish towels, and let the rolls sit in a warm, draft-free location until they have doubled in size, about 1 hour. Preheat the oven to 400°F. Bake the rolls for 10 minutes, or until golden brown.

TIP   If you know you are going to freeze the uncooked rolls, use 3 packages yeast. After cutting the rolls and placing them in muffin tins, cover the tins with foil and freeze them for up to 3 months. (Do not let them rise in the tins before freezing.) Three hours before serving, remove the rolls from the freezer, and remove and discard the foil. Cover the muffin tins lightly with dish towels, and put them in a warm place to rise. (We put them on top of the clothes dryer and run a cycle to warm them up!) Bake according to the directions above.

Makes about 30 rolls

✴ Mushrooms and Rice

Mother always said she could eat this dish every night, and we could too.

NOW

4 to 6 green onions (scallions), finely chopped

Two 10³/₄-ounce cans beef consommé (2²/₃ cups)

2 tablespoons soy sauce

¹/₃ cup salad oil

¹/₂ teaspoon salt

LATER

2²/₃ cups instant rice

One 8-ounce can mushrooms, drained

NOW

Put the chopped green onions in an airtight container and refrigerate them. In a separate bowl, combine the consommé, soy sauce, salad oil, and salt, and mix well. Cover and refrigerate for up to 24 hours.

LATER

Preheat the oven to 350°F. Grease a 2-quart casserole dish and add the rice. Scatter the mushrooms and the green onions over the rice and pour the consommé mixture over it all. Mix well. Cover the casserole with a lid or aluminum foil and bake for no more than 30 to 45 minutes, until all the liquid is absorbed. Do not stir the casserole while it is baking.

Serves 6

Peruvian Rice

This adds a truly new twist to plain old rice. Try serving it with Beef Brisket (page 143).

1 cup sour cream
One 4-ounce can diced green chiles
2 cups grated Monterey Jack cheese (about 8 ounces)
2 cups cooked rice

NOW

Grease a 1½-quart baking dish. In a medium bowl, combine the sour cream, chiles, and cheese. Layer 1 cup of the rice in the prepared baking dish. Top with a layer of one-half of the cheese mixture. Repeat the rice and cheese layers. Cover and refrigerate for several hours or overnight.

LATER

Remove the rice mixture from the refrigerator, and let it sit for up to 1 hour. Preheat the oven to 350°F. Bake for 30 to 40 minutes, until bubbly.

TIP If you like your rice spicy, use Pepper Jack cheese in place of the Monterey Jack. If you like it super spicy, use diced jalapeños instead of the green chiles.

Serves 4

✳ Green and Yellow Rice

This dish is incredibly popular. It goes particularly well with Stew Brazil (page 179).

3 cups cooked rice
$1/4$ cup butter or margarine ($1/2$ stick), melted
1 cup milk
4 eggs, lightly beaten
1 pound sharp cheddar cheese, grated (4 cups)
One 10-ounce package frozen chopped spinach, cooked and drained
1 tablespoon chopped onion
1 tablespoon Worcestershire sauce
$1/2$ teaspoon dried marjoram
$1/2$ teaspoon dried thyme
$1/2$ teaspoon dried rosemary
$1/2$ teaspoon salt

NOW

In a medium bowl, combine the rice and butter, and mix well. In a large bowl, beat the milk and eggs together with a whisk. Add the cheese and spinach, and mix well. Stir in the onion, Worcestershire sauce, marjoram, thyme, rosemary, and salt. Add the rice mixture, and mix well. Transfer to a 2-quart baking dish. Cover and refrigerate for up to 24 hours.

LATER

Preheat the oven to 350°F. Set the baking dish in a pan of warm water, and bake the casserole for 45 minutes.

Serves 6

Fried Rice

This superb rice casserole is a wonderful side dish, but it can easily be made into a main dish by adding cooked shrimp, chicken, ham, or turkey.

NOW

6 to 8 green onions (scallions), finely chopped

1 generous cup finely chopped celery

2 tablespoons vegetable oil

2 cups cooked rice

1 pinch of salt

2 to 3 tablespoons soy sauce

LATER

$^1/_2$ cup slivered almonds

1 tablespoon butter

NOW

In a large skillet over medium heat, cook the green onions and celery in the oil for about 3 to 5 minutes, until softened but not browned. Add the rice, salt, and soy sauce, mix well, and transfer to a 2-quart baking dish. Cover and refrigerate for 3 hours or up to 24 hours.

LATER

Preheat the oven to 350°F. Bake, uncovered, for about 30 minutes, or until thoroughly heated. In a small skillet over medium heat, cook the almonds in the butter until they turn golden brown. Transfer them to paper towels to drain. Sprinkle the toasted almonds on top of the casserole just before serving.

Serves 4

Mexican Rice

This is our favorite side dish for any Mexican meal, especially served with Cinco de Mayo Beef (page 145). The recipe is easy to double for large parties.

1 large onion, finely chopped
¼ cup vegetable oil
1 tablespoon crushed garlic
2 cups long-grained white rice
One 14½-ounce can peeled and diced tomatoes
3 cans beef consommé, undiluted (about 4 cups)
2 teaspoons ground cumin
1 package (1¼ ounces) taco seasoning

NOW

In a large saucepan over medium heat, cook the onion in the oil until tender but not browned, 3 to 5 minutes. Add the garlic and rice, and cook another 3 to 5 minutes, stirring often, until the rice is pale yellow. Add the tomatoes, consommé, cumin, and taco seasoning. Bring to a boil over high heat. Cover, reduce the heat to low, and simmer until the liquid has been absorbed and the rice is tender, about 20 minutes. Transfer to a microwave-safe dish. Cover and refrigerate for up to 3 days.

LATER

Reheat in the microwave for 3½ minutes on high. Stir to make sure the rice is hot.

Serves 8

Curried Noodles

These yummy noodles go well with poultry, seafood, barbecued meat, or any simple meat dish.

1 pound medium-wide noodles
$1/2$ cup butter (1 stick)
$1/4$ cup all-purpose flour
1 tablespoon curry powder
2 teaspoons salt
$1/2$ teaspoon pepper
$41/2$ cups milk
1 cup sour cream
$3/4$ cup prepared mango chutney

NOW

Grease a 3-quart baking dish, and set aside. Cook the noodles according to the package directions. Drain, rinse, and set aside.

Melt the butter in a large saucepan over medium heat. Whisk in the flour, curry powder, salt, and pepper. Gradually stir in the milk and bring it to a boil. Keep whisking until the sauce has thickened, then remove it from the heat and add the sour cream and chutney. Add the noodles and mix well. Transfer the noodles and their sauce to the prepared baking dish. Cover and refrigerate for 3 hours or up to 2 days.

LATER

Preheat the oven to 350°F. Bake, covered, for 30 to 45 minutes, until bubbly.

Serves 8

✳ Norfolk Noodles

A very tasty dish that is great served with No Work Chicken (page 163)
or Party Chicken (page 166).

NOW

12 ounces wide noodles

1 cup finely chopped fresh parsley

2 cups large-curd cottage cheese

2 cups sour cream

1 tablespoon Worcestershire sauce

1 dash of hot pepper sauce

6 to 8 green onions (scallions), chopped

LATER

4 ounces grated sharp cheddar cheese (1 cup)

$1/2$ teaspoon paprika

NOW

Prepare the noodles according to the directions on the package. Drain them, and transfer to a large bowl. Add the parsley, cottage cheese, sour cream, Worcestershire sauce, hot pepper sauce, and onions, and mix well. Transfer to a shallow, 3-quart baking dish. Cover and refrigerate, for up to 3 days.

LATER

Preheat the oven to 350°F. Sprinkle the cheese on top, and then the paprika. Bake, uncovered, for 40 minutes until the noodles are thoroughly heated and the cheese has melted.

Serves 8

The Ultimate Potato Casserole

This recipe has everything we love on top of potatoes!

1 whole garlic bulb
1$^1/_2$ teaspoons olive oil
4 pounds red potatoes, peeled and cut into large pieces
8 slices bacon
8 green onions (scallions), thinly sliced
2 cups sour cream
$^1/_2$ cup butter (1 stick)
2 cups grated cheddar cheese, divided
$^1/_2$ cup milk
1 teaspoon salt
$^1/_2$ teaspoon pepper

NOW

Preheat the oven to 425°F. Grease a 9 x 13-inch baking dish, and set aside. Cut off the pointed end of the garlic bulb, and drizzle the olive oil over the cut end. Wrap the bulb in aluminum foil, and bake it for 30 minutes, or until tender. Remove from the oven, open the foil, and set aside to cool. Boil the potatoes in a large pot of salted water until tender, about 20 minutes, or until you can easily pierce them with a fork. Drain and return to the pot.

In a large skillet over medium-high heat, fry the bacon until it is crisp. Remove it from the skillet, and drain on paper towels. Add the green onions to the bacon drippings in the skillet, and cook, stirring frequently, until tender, about 5 minutes. Set aside.

Squeeze the roasted garlic into the hot potatoes, and beat with an electric beater until smooth. Add the sour cream, butter, 1 cup of the cheese, milk, salt, and pepper, and mix well. Transfer to the prepared baking dish, and top with the remaining 1 cup cheese. Cover and refrigerate for 3 hours or overnight.

LATER

Remove the baking dish from the refrigerator, and let the casserole sit for 20 to 30 minutes. Preheat the oven to 350°F. Bake, uncovered, for 35 to 45 minutes, until thoroughly heated.

Serves 8 to 10

Great Grate Potatoes

This is our most often used, most often requested potato recipe.

8 to 10 large red potatoes, skin on
2 cups whipping or heavy cream
Onion salt
Salt and pepper
2 tablespoons butter, cut into small pieces

NOW

Grease a 9 x 13-inch baking dish, and set aside. Cook the potatoes in a large pot of boiling water until tender, about 30 minutes, or until you can easily pierce them with a fork. Drain and return to the pot until cool enough to handle. Peel and grate the potatoes into the prepared baking dish. Pour the cream over the potatoes. Season with the onion salt, and add salt and pepper to taste. Dot with the butter. Cover and refrigerate for 3 hours or overnight.

LATER
Preheat the oven to 350°F. Bake the casserole, uncovered, for about 40 minutes, until the potatoes are lightly browned and bubbly.

•• ••

TIP   For variety, you can toss the grated potatoes with grated red onion or 1 cup grated cheddar cheese before adding the cream. Also, the leftovers are great fried for breakfast.

•• ••

Serves 8 to 10

✳ Stuffed Baked Potatoes

These are great to have on hand in the freezer. Of course, they go particularly well with hearty meat dishes, such as Saucy Pork Chops (page 178) or Baby Back Ribs (page 181).

> 4 baking potatoes (about ¹/₂ pound each)
> 2 tablespoons margarine or bacon drippings, softened
> 2 tablespoons margarine, cut into small pieces
> ¹/₃ cup milk
> 1 egg, lightly beaten
> 4 ounces cheddar cheese, grated (1 cup)
> 2 tablespoons chopped chives, fresh or freeze-dried
> Salt and pepper
> Paprika

NOW

Preheat the oven to 425°F. Wash the potatoes well, dry them, then rub them lightly with the softened margarine or bacon grease. Bake for 1 hour until tender. Remove the potatoes from the oven, and let them cool enough to handle. Cut them in half lengthwise. Carefully scoop out most of the pulp of the potato, leaving the skins intact. Place the skins on a baking sheet, and set aside.

Transfer the pulp to a large bowl. Add the margarine pieces, milk, and egg, and beat with an electric mixer until smooth (no lumps!). Add the cheese and chives, season with salt and pepper to taste, and mix well. Carefully transfer the pulp mixture back into the skins. Arrange the stuffed potatoes on a baking sheet, and sprinkle with paprika. Freeze thoroughly. When frozen, transfer the stuffed potatoes to an airtight container, and return them to the freezer for up to 3 months.

LATER

Allow the potatoes to thaw in the refrigerator overnight. Preheat the oven to 350°F. Bake for 25 minutes, until the very top of the potato filling begins to turn golden brown.

Serves 8

Fluffy Mashed Potato Casserole

No last-minute mashing with this dish.

NOW
2 cups mashed potatoes
1 cup cream cheese (8 ounces), softened
1 small onion, finely chopped
2 eggs, lightly beaten
2 tablespoons all-purpose flour
Salt and pepper

LATER
One 2.8-ounce can French-fried onions

NOW

In a large bowl, combine the potatoes, cream cheese, onion, eggs, and flour. With an electric beater on medium speed, mix until blended. Increase the speed to high, and beat the potato mixture until it's light and fluffy. Season with salt and pepper, and mix well. Cover and refrigerate for 3 hours or up to 2 days.

LATER

Remove the potato mixture from the refrigerator, and let it sit for up to 1 hour. Preheat the oven to 325°F. Put the potato mixture in a greased 3-quart casserole dish. Spread the French-fried onions on top of the potato mixture, and bake for 30 to 40 minutes, until bubbly.

Serves 4

Cheesy Dilled Potatoes

This is a nice twist on escalloped potatoes.

> 2 pounds large baking potatoes, peeled and thinly sliced
> $^1/_2$ cup cooked and crumbled bacon
> 1 medium onion, thinly sliced
> 3 tablespoons butter
> 3 tablespoons flour
> $^1/_2$ teaspoon seasoned salt
> $^1/_2$ teaspoon white pepper
> $^1/_4$ teaspoon dill seed
> $1^3/_4$ cups milk
> 4 ounces sharp cheddar cheese, grated (1 cup)

NOW

Grease a shallow 2-quart baking dish. Layer the potatoes, bacon, and onion in the dish. Melt the butter in a saucepan over medium heat. Whisk in the flour, seasoned salt, white pepper, and dill seed. Cook, stirring frequently, until the sauce begins to bubble. Slowly add the milk, whisking constantly, until the sauce thickens. Add the cheese and stir until it melts. Pour the sauce over the potatoes. Cover and refrigerate for up to 8 hours.

LATER

Preheat the oven to 350°F. Bake the casserole, covered, for 45 minutes. Uncover, and bake 15 minutes more, until casserole is bubbly and browned.

 TIP Leftovers are terrific fried for breakfast.

Serves 6 to 8

Baked Potato Dressing

This special dressing makes something great out of a plain baked potato. It is a nice topping for other vegetables too, such as green beans or broccoli.

NOW
$^1/_2$ cup butter (1 stick), softened
4 ounces cheddar cheese, grated (1 cup)
$^1/_2$ cup sour cream
2 green onions (scallions), finely chopped
$^1/_4$ cup crumbled cooked bacon or canned bacon bits

LATER
6 baked potatoes

NOW
In a medium bowl, combine the butter, cheese, sour cream, green onions, and bacon, and mix well. Cover and refrigerate for up to 5 days.

LATER
Remove the dressing from the refrigerator and let it sit for 20 to 30 minutes. Mix well, and serve as a topping for the baked potatoes.

Serves 6

Sweet Potato Casserole

This is our Thanksgiving offering of sweet potatoes.

3 cups cooked and mashed sweet potatoes (or canned sweet potatoes)
$^1/_2$ cup sugar
2 eggs, lightly beaten
$^1/_3$ cup milk
1 teaspoon vanilla
$^1/_2$ cup butter (1 stick), melted
$^1/_4$ cup all-purpose flour
2 tablespoons butter, softened
$^1/_2$ cup firmly packed dark brown sugar
$^1/_2$ cup chopped pecans

NOW

Grease a 2-quart baking dish. In a large bowl, combine the sweet potatoes, sugar, eggs, milk, vanilla, and melted butter. Mix well, transfer to the prepared baking dish, and set aside.

In a small bowl, with a pastry blender, combine the flour, softened butter, and brown sugar, mixing until crumbly. Add the pecans, mix well, and sprinkle over the sweet potato mixture. Cover and refrigerate for up to 2 days.

LATER

Preheat the oven to 350°F. Bake, uncovered, for 35 to 45 minutes, until very lightly browned and crusty.

Serves 6 to 8

Bossa Nova Baked Beans

These are a great change from regular baked beans. The chili, brown sugar, and cumin give them their zippy bossa nova flavor.

One 16-ounce can baked beans
One 15-ounce can chili with beans
One 15-ounce can chili beans or pinto beans
One 8-ounce can tomato sauce
1 small onion, finely chopped
$1/4$ cup firmly packed dark brown sugar
1 tablespoon ground cumin
1 teaspoon garlic salt
4 ounces Monterey Jack cheese, grated (1 cup)

NOW

Grease a 2-quart baking dish. Combine all the ingredients in a large bowl, and mix well. Transfer the bean mixture to the prepared baking dish. Cover and refrigerate for 3 hours or up to 2 days.

LATER

Preheat the oven to 325°F. Bake the bean mixture, uncovered, for 1 hour, until bubbly.

Serves 6

Marcia's Beans

These were Mother's favorite baked beans, but as much as we'd love to know, we still haven't discovered who Marcia is! This recipe never appeared in Mother's books—it's from her personal recipe files.

Two 28-ounce cans baked beans
2 large Granny Smith apples (or other tart, firm apples), peeled and grated
2 tablespoons butter, cut into small pieces
$1/2$ cup firmly packed dark brown sugar,
6 slices bacon, diced and partially cooked, or $1/2$ cup bacon bits

NOW

Grease a 3-quart baking dish. Combine all the ingredients in a large bowl, and mix well. Transfer to the prepared baking dish. Cover, and refrigerate for 3 hours or overnight.

LATER

Preheat the oven to 250°F. Bake the bean mixture, uncovered, for 2 hours.

Serves 8

Best Bean Casserole

Even people who say they hate beans will be licking the bowl clean!

6 slices bacon
1 large onion, finely chopped
1 large green bell pepper, finely chopped
One 28-ounce can baked beans
One 16-ounce can pinto beans, drained
One 16-ounce can kidney beans, drained
Two 10-ounce packages frozen French-cut green beans, thawed and
    drained
1 cup firmly packed dark brown sugar
One 12-ounce jar chili sauce

NOW

Grease a 3-quart baking dish, and set aside. In a medium skillet over medium-high heat, fry the bacon until crisp. Remove from the skillet and drain on paper towels. Add the onion and bell pepper to the bacon drippings in the skillet, and cook, stirring frequently until the vegetables are just beginning to become tender, 3 to 5 minutes. Transfer the vegetables to a large bowl. Crumble the bacon and add it to the vegetables. Add the canned beans (all three varieties), green beans, sugar, and chili sauce, and mix well. Transfer to the prepared baking dish. Cover, and refrigerate for 3 hours or overnight.

LATER

Preheat the oven to 350°F. Bake the casserole, uncovered, for 1 hour, until it is browned and most of the liquid has evaporated.

Serves 12

Swiss Beans

This is a tried-and-true family recipe.

Two 10-ounce packages frozen French-cut green beans, thawed and
   drained
3 tablespoons butter, melted, divided
1 tablespoon flour
$^1/_2$ teaspoon salt
$^1/_8$ teaspoon pepper
$^1/_2$ teaspoon sugar
$^1/_4$ cup milk
$^1/_2$ small onion, finely chopped
1 cup sour cream
6 ounces Swiss cheese, grated (1$^1/_2$ cups)
1 cup crushed cornflakes cereal

NOW

Grease a 1$^1/_2$-quart baking dish, add the green beans, and set aside. In a
small saucepan over medium heat, whisk together 2 tablespoons of the
melted butter, the flour, salt, pepper, and sugar. Cook, stirring frequently,
until bubbly. Whisk in the milk. Remove from heat and stir in the onion
and sour cream. Spread the sauce over the top of the green beans. Top with
the grated cheese.

In a small bowl, combine the cornflakes with the remaining 1 tablespoon
melted butter. Spread on top of the green bean mixture. Cover and
refrigerate for 3 hours or overnight.

MAKE IT NOW, BAKE IT LATER!

LATER
Preheat the oven to 400°F. Bake the casserole, uncovered, for 20 to 25 minutes, until bubbly.

TIP Cheddar cheese works well in place of the Swiss.

Serves 6 to 8

Green Bean Classique

Here's a spin on the classic green bean casserole. The water chestnuts and bean sprouts add just the right amount of crunch.

NOW
Three 10-ounce packages frozen French-cut green beans, thawed and
    drained
One 5-ounce can water chestnuts, diced
8 ounces bean sprouts
One 4-ounce can sliced mushrooms, drained
Two 10^3/$_4$-ounce cans cream of celery soup
^{1}/$_2$ cup milk
1 teaspoon salt
^{1}/$_2$ teaspoon pepper

LATER

One 6-ounce can French-fried onions

NOW

Grease a 2-quart baking dish. In a medium bowl, combine the green beans, water chestnuts, sprouts, and mushrooms, and mix well. Transfer the vegetables to the prepared baking dish.

In another medium bowl, combine the soup, milk, salt, and pepper, mixing until smooth. Pour the soup mixture over the vegetables. Cover and refrigerate for 3 hours or overnight.

LATER

Preheat the oven to 325°F. Bake the casserole, uncovered, for 50 minutes, until bubbly. Cover the top of the casserole with the French-fried onions. Bake for 10 minutes more, until lightly browned.

Serves 12 to 15

Spinach for Guys

Big, famous steakhouses serve spinach side dishes such as this one. Now you have a recipe that's even better.

Two 10-ounce packages frozen chopped spinach, thawed
2 tablespoons chopped onion
$1/4$ cup butter ($1/2$ stick)
2 tablespoons flour
One 5-ounce can evaporated milk
8 ounces pepper-jack cheese, grated (2 cups)
$1/2$ teaspoon pepper
$3/4$ teaspoon garlic salt
$1/2$ teaspoon salt
1 teaspoon Worcestershire sauce
1 dash of hot pepper sauce
1 cup plain breadcrumbs
1 tablespoon butter, melted

NOW

Butter a 2-quart baking dish, and set aside. Squeeze as much of the liquid from the spinach as possible, reserving $1/2$ cup of the liquid. Set the spinach and reserved liquid aside. In a large skillet over medium heat, cook the onion in the butter until the onion has softened, 3 to 5 minutes. Add the flour and mix well. Slowly stir in the evaporated milk and the reserved spinach liquid, and mix well. Stir in the cheese, pepper, garlic salt, salt, Worcestershire sauce, and hot pepper sauce. Mix well.

Continue cooking until the cheese has melted, then add the reserved spinach and mix well. Pour the spinach mixture into the prepared baking dish. In a small bowl, combine the breadcrumbs and melted butter. Spread on top of the spinach mixture. Cover and refrigerate for 3 hours or overnight.

LATER

Preheat the oven to 375°F. Bake, uncovered, for 25 to 30 minutes, until bubbly.

Serves 6 to 8

✳ Simple Spinach

This recipe will make you like your spinach!

NOW
Two 10-ounce packages frozen chopped spinach
1 cup sour cream
1 envelope (1½ ounces) dehydrated onion soup
1 dash of hot pepper sauce
Salt and pepper

LATER
¼ cup chopped almonds

NOW
Spray a 9 x 9-inch baking dish with vegetable cooking spray, and set aside. Cook the spinach as directed on the package, using the minimum cooking time. Drain well.

In a medium bowl, combine the spinach, sour cream, soup mix, and hot pepper sauce, mixing well. Season with salt and pepper to taste. Transfer to the prepared baking dish. Cover and refrigerate for up to 24 hours.

LATER
Preheat the oven to 350°F. Bake the casserole, uncovered, for 20 minutes. Sprinkle the almonds on top, and bake 15 minutes more, until the almonds are lightly browned.

Serves 4 to 6

Cheesy Broccoli

We bet that none of the top government officials who say they hate broccoli ever tried our version!

1 medium onion, finely chopped
$^1/_2$ cup butter or margarine (1 stick), divided
One 10$^3/_4$-ounce can cream of celery soup
One 4-ounce can chopped mushrooms, drained
8 ounces Velveeta or cheddar cheese, grated or cut into small pieces (2 cups)
1 clove garlic, minced
Two 10-ounce packages frozen chopped broccoli, thawed and drained
Salt and pepper
2 cups Pepperidge Farm herb seasoned stuffing mix, crushed

NOW

Lightly grease a 3-quart baking dish, and set aside. In a large saucepan over medium heat, cook the onion in $^1/_4$ cup of the butter until tender. Add the soup, mushrooms, cheese, garlic, and broccoli. Season with salt and pepper to taste, and mix well. Transfer to the prepared baking dish. Combine the stuffing with the remaining $^1/_4$ cup butter, and mix well. Crumble the stuffing mixture over the broccoli mixture. Cover and refrigerate for up to 24 hours.

LATER

Preheat the oven to 350°F. Bake the casserole, uncovered, for 30 to 45 minutes, until bubbly.

TIP Pep up this casserole with Mexican Velveeta or cheddar with jalapeños.

Serves 10 to 15

Broccoli Vinaigrette

This tasty cold dish can also be served as a starter, with toothpicks.

1 cup vegetable oil
$1/3$ cup red wine vinegar
$1/3$ cup lemon juice
1 tablespoon sugar
$1^1/2$ teaspoons salt
$1^1/2$ teaspoons paprika
$1^1/2$ teaspoons dry mustard
1 teaspoon dried crumbled oregano
$1/8$ teaspoon cayenne pepper
$2/3$ cup finely chopped dill pickles
$2/3$ cup minced red bell pepper
$1/3$ cup finely chopped parsley
$1/4$ cup capers ($2^1/2$ ounces), optional
2 pounds broccoli florets, broken into bite-sized pieces

NOW

In a large jar, combine the oil, vinegar, lemon juice, sugar, salt, paprika, dry mustard, oregano, cayenne, pickles, bell pepper, and parsley. Add the capers, if desired. Shake vigorously to combine. Put the broccoli in an airtight container, and pour in the vinaigrette. Cover tightly and shake well to coat all the broccoli. Chill overnight or up to 5 days, tossing occasionally.

LATER

Drain the broccoli mixture, reserving the solids from the vinaigrette in the bottom of the strainer. Arrange the broccoli on a platter, and sprinkle with the reserved solids from the vinaigrette.

Serves 6

Fabulous Carrot Casserole

Our most requested carrot recipe.

3 cups sliced carrots
12 saltine crackers, crushed
2 tablespoons butter
1 tablespoon minced onion
$^{1}/_{2}$ teaspoon pepper
4 ounces cheddar cheese, grated (1 cup)

NOW

Grease a $1^{1}/_{2}$-quart baking dish, and set aside. Cook the carrots in boiling water until tender. Drain, reserving $^{2}/_{3}$ cup of the cooking liquid. Mash the carrots. In a large bowl, combine the mashed carrots, reserved carrot liquid, crackers, butter, onion, pepper, and cheese, and mix well. Transfer to the prepared baking dish. Cover and refrigerate for 3 hours or overnight.

LATER

Preheat the oven to 350°F. Bake the casserole, uncovered, for 30 to 35 minutes, or until it is bubbly and the cheese melts.

Serves 4 to 6

"Puttin' On the Ritz" Carrots

*Carrots may not seem very upscale, but this dish elevates them to a new
level.*

2 pounds carrots, peeled and thinly sliced
$^1/_2$ teaspoon salt
$^1/_2$ cup mayonnaise
2 tablespoons dried chopped or minced onions
1 tablespoon prepared horseradish
1 cup crushed Ritz crackers
$^1/_4$ cup butter ($^1/_2$ stick), melted

NOW

Grease a shallow, 2-quart baking dish, and set aside. Put the carrots in a
medium saucepan and barely cover them with water. Add the salt and cook
on medium for 15 to 20 minutes, until a fork can be easily inserted into a
carrot slice. Drain the carrots, reserving $^1/_3$ cup of the cooking liquid.
Transfer the carrots to the prepared baking dish.

In a small bowl, combine the mayonnaise, onions, horseradish, and
reserved carrot liquid, mixing until smooth. Spread the sauce over the
carrots. Top with the crushed crackers, and drizzle melted butter over all.
Cover and refrigerate for several hours or overnight.

LATER

Preheat the oven to 350°F. Bake the casserole, uncovered, for 30 minutes,
until bubbly and lightly browned.

Serves 4 to 6

✳ Colorful Carrots

In Mother's estimation, this is a must-have side dish for any barbecue.

1½ pounds carrots
1 medium green bell pepper, cut into thin strips
1 medium yellow onion, thinly sliced and separated into rings
One 10¾-ounce can tomato soup
1 cup sugar
⅓ cup vegetable oil
¾ cup vinegar
1 tablespoon salt
1 tablespoon freshly ground black pepper

NOW

Peel the carrots and slice them lengthwise into thin strips about 4 inches long. Cook the carrots in boiling water until tender but still crisp, 10 to 15 minutes. Drain and spread on the bottom of an 8 x 12-inch baking dish. Layer the bell pepper and onion on top, and set aside.

In a medium saucepan over medium heat, combine the soup, sugar, oil, vinegar, salt, and pepper. Stirring frequently, bring to a boil. Immediately pour the soup mixture over the vegetables. Allow it to cool, cover, and refrigerate for up to 2 weeks.

LATER

Serve cold.

Serves 8

Celery Celebration

The nuts give this dish its backbone. It is particularly tasty served with Barbecued Butterflied Lamb (page 183).

NOW
4 cups sliced celery
$1/4$ cup minced onion
$1/2$ cup water
$1/2$ teaspoon salt
One $10^{3}/4$-ounce can cream of celery soup
$1/2$ cup chopped pecans
$1/4$ cup crumbled bacon

LATER
1 cup buttery cracker crumbs
$1/4$ cup butter ($1/2$ stick), cut into small pieces

NOW

Grease a 1-quart baking dish, and set aside. In a medium saucepan over high heat, combine the celery, onion, water, and salt, and bring to a boil. Cover, reduce the heat to medium-low, and let simmer for 5 minutes. Drain. Add the soup, pecans, and bacon, and mix well. Transfer to the prepared baking dish. Cover and refrigerate for 3 hours or overnight.

LATER

Preheat the oven to 350°F. Top with the cracker crumbs and dot with the butter. Cover and bake for 20 minutes. Then uncover and bake for 10 minutes more, until bubbly and lightly browned.

Serves 4 to 6

Tomatoes Vinaigrette

The wonderful, fresh tomatoes you can get from farm stands and farmers' markets in late summer and early fall are perfect for this dish, but the recipe is good throughout the year. The olives add color.

NOW
4 large tomatoes, sliced into ½-inch slices
¼ cup finely chopped parsley
⅓ cup olive oil
3 tablespoons red wine vinegar
1 teaspoon salt
1 teaspoon pepper
¼ cup finely chopped basil

LATER
One 15-ounce can whole ripe pitted olives, drained

NOW

Arrange the tomato slices on a serving dish, and set aside. In a small bowl, combine the parsley, olive oil, vinegar, salt, pepper, and basil, and mix well. Drizzle the vinaigrette over the tomatoes, making sure to get some on each slice. Cover and refrigerate for at least 2 hours or up to 3 days.

LATER

Scatter the olives over the tomatoes and serve cold or at room temperature.

Serves 6 to 8

Parsley Dressing for Fresh Tomatoes

The parsley and pickles make this dressing entirely different from most, and it can be made days ahead.

2 cups finely chopped parsley
$1/2$ cup finely chopped chives
1 cup finely chopped dill or sweet pickles
2 cloves garlic
Salt and pepper
$1/2$ cup olive oil
$1/2$ cup red wine vinegar
$1/4$ cup tarragon vinegar

NOW

Combine all the ingredients in a food processor, pulsing until very finely chopped. (Do not puree.) Transfer to a jar, cover tightly, and let sit at room temperature for 2 days. Then, refrigerate for up to 2 weeks.

LATER

Mix well before serving ice cold over chilled, peeled, and sliced tomatoes.

Makes enough for 12 to 14 large tomatoes

Vegetable Medley

This cold side dish offers great contrasting flavors.

NOW
Two 15-ounce cans cut whole green beans, drained
One 5-ounce can sliced water chestnuts, drained
One 12-ounce jar marinated artichoke hearts, drained and cut in half
1 large red onion, coarsely chopped
$1/2$ pound sliced fresh mushrooms
1 cup vegetable oil
$1/2$ cup red wine vinegar
1 tablespoon dill weed
1 teaspoon dried crumbled oregano
1 teaspoon dry mustard
Salt and pepper

LATER
1 small red bell pepper, finely diced

NOW
In a large bowl, combine the green beans, water chestnuts, artichoke hearts, onion, and mushrooms. In a small bowl, combine the oil, vinegar, dill, oregano, and dry mustard. Season with salt and pepper to taste, mix well, and drizzle over the vegetables. Stir and cover well. Refrigerate for at least 4 hours or up to 1 week, stirring occasionally. (It is best refrigerated at least overnight.)

LATER
Drain and put in a serving dish, and scatter the bell pepper on top.

Serves 6 to 8

Garden Basket

Commercial Italian dressings make terrific marinades for vegetables and barbecued meats. This vegetable combination is superb.

1 cup thinly sliced carrots

4 stalks celery, thinly sliced

1 small red onion, cut into thin rings

2 cups bite-sized cauliflower florets

One 10-ounce package frozen artichoke hearts, cooked, cut in half, and
   chilled

1 cup Italian dressing

1 cup mayonnaise

1 teaspoon dill weed

2 tablespoons chili sauce

1 tablespoon lemon juice

1/2 teaspoon salt

NOW

In a large bowl, combine the carrots, celery, onion, cauliflower, artichoke hearts, and Italian dressing. Mix well and refrigerate for 2 to 4 hours. In a small bowl, combine the mayonnaise, dill, chili sauce, lemon juice, and salt. Mix well and pour over vegetables, stirring until all the vegetables are coated with the mayonnaise mixture. Cover tightly and refrigerate overnight or up to 3 days.

LATER

Toss to distribute the dressing again, and serve cold.

Serves 4 to 6

Curried Fruit

We love to serve this at brunches, but it's wonderful with grilled meats too.

NOW
Two 15-ounce cans sliced peaches
Two 15-ounce cans sliced pears
Two 15-ounce cans apricots
Two 10-ounce cans pineapple chunks
One 10-ounce jar maraschino cherries
$1/2$ cup butter (1 stick)
$1/2$ cup firmly packed dark brown sugar
2 to 3 teaspoons curry powder

LATER
$1/2$ cup slivered almonds

NOW

Grease a 9 x 13-inch baking dish. Place the fruits in a colander, and drain them well. Mix well, transfer the fruit to the prepared baking dish, and set aside. Melt the butter in a small saucepan over medium heat. Add the brown sugar and curry powder, and mix well. Drizzle the sauce over the fruit. Cover and refrigerate for 3 hours or overnight.

LATER

Remove the curried fruit from refrigerator, and let it sit for 20 to 30 minutes. Preheat the oven to 325°F. In a small, dry skillet over medium heat, toast the almonds until lightly browned, and set aside. Bake the fruit for 45 minutes, until lightly browned. Top with the almonds, and bake 15 minutes more.

Serves 8 to 10

Layered Onion Rings

This is terrific to serve with simple chicken dishes, such as No Work Chicken (page 163).

6 tablespoons butter ($^3/_4$ stick), divided
4 large onions, sliced into $^1/_4$-inch rings
1 teaspoon dried thyme
One 10$^3/_4$-ounce can cream of chicken soup
$^1/_2$ cup milk
8 ounces Swiss cheese, grated (2 cups)
6 slices French bread, about 1 inch thick

NOW

Grease a 2-quart baking dish, and set aside. In a large skillet over medium-high heat, melt 3 tablespoons of the butter. Add the onions and cook just until they begin to get tender, 3 to 5 minutes. Stir in the thyme, and set aside. In a small bowl, combine the soup and milk, and set aside.

In the prepared baking dish, layer one-half of the onions, one-half of the soup mixture, and one-half of the cheese. Repeat the layers. Butter one side of each slice of bread with the remaining 3 tablespoons butter, and place buttered-side up on top of the casserole. Cover, and refrigerate for 3 hours or overnight.

LATER

Preheat the oven to 350°F. Bake the casserole, uncovered, for 30 minutes until bubbly and golden brown.

Serves 6 to 8

Mexican Corn Quiche

This marvelous side dish complements all kinds of main dishes, not just Mexican. Try it with Baby Back Ribs (page 181).

5 eggs, lightly beaten
1/4 cup all-purpose flour
1/2 teaspoon baking powder
1 dash of salt
1/4 cup butter (1/2 stick), melted
One 4-ounce can diced green chiles
1 cup small-curd cottage cheese
One 15-ounce can cream-style corn
8 ounces Monterey Jack cheese, grated (2 cups)

NOW

Preheat the oven to 400°F. Grease a 9 x 9-inch baking dish, and set aside. In a large bowl, combine the eggs, flour, baking powder, and salt, and mix well. Add the butter, chiles, cottage cheese, corn, and cheese, and mix well. Transfer to the prepared baking dish. Bake for 15 minutes, and reduce heat to 350°F. Bake for 35 to 40 minutes more, until the quiche is puffed and lightly browned. Allow to cool, cover, and refrigerate for up to 3 days.

LATER

Preheat the oven to 350°F. Bake for 20 minutes, until thoroughly heated.

TIP This quiche can also be cut into small squares and served as a starter. It will make about 36 canapés.

Serves 6 to 8

MAKE IT NOW, BAKE IT LATER!

Mushroom Casserole

If you are a mushroom lover, this dish is for you.

1/4 cup butter (1/2 stick) plus 3 tablespoons, softened
1 pound sliced mushrooms, coarsely chopped
6 slices white bread, crusts removed
1 cup finely chopped onion
1 cup finely chopped celery
1 cup finely chopped green bell pepper
1/2 cup mayonnaise
Salt and pepper
2 eggs
1 1/2 cups milk

NOW

Grease a 2-quart baking dish, and set aside. Melt 1/4 cup of the butter in a medium skillet over medium-high heat, and add the mushrooms. Cook, stirring frequently, until the mushrooms have softened and most of their liquid has evaporated. Set aside.

Spread about 1/2 tablespoon of the softened butter on each slice of bread. Cut the bread slices into 1-inch squares, and arrange one-half of the bread squares in the bottom of the dish. In a medium bowl, combine the cooked mushrooms, onions, celery, bell pepper, and mayonnaise, and mix well. Season with salt and pepper to taste. Spread the mushroom mixture over the bread and top with the remaining bread squares. In a small bowl, beat the eggs and milk together, and pour them over the mushroom mixture. Cover and refrigerate for 2 hours or overnight.

LATER

Preheat the oven to 325°F. Bake the casserole, uncovered, for 1 hour, until bubbly and lightly browned.

Serves 6 to 8

English Peas

These are a winner! The crunchy topping makes this dish really special.

10 tablespoons butter (1 stick plus 2 tablespoons), melted, divided
1 cup finely chopped celery
1 cup finely chopped onion
$^1/_2$ cup finely chopped green bell pepper
2 cups frozen peas, thawed and drained (we use petite peas)
One 5-ounce can water chestnuts, diced
One 2-ounce jar diced pimientos
One 10$^3/_4$-ounce can cream of celery soup
1 cup crushed cornflakes cereal

NOW

Grease a 2-quart baking dish, and set aside. In a large bowl, combine $^1/_2$ cup of the melted butter with the celery, onion, bell pepper, peas, water chestnuts, pimientos, and soup. Mix well, and transfer to the prepared baking dish. In a small bowl, combine the cornflakes and the remaining 2 tablespoons melted butter. Mix well, and spread on top of the pea mixture. Cover and refrigerate for 3 hours or overnight.

LATER

Preheat the oven to 350°F. Bake the casserole, uncovered, for 30 to 45 minutes, until bubbly.

TIP If you need to serve 10 people, just double the peas and soup in the recipe.

Serves 4 to 6

Zucchini and Green Chiles

Legend has it that early explorers brought squash seeds back to Europe from the New World, and from those seeds came the zucchini we know so well today. Whatever its origin, this great side dish shows that zucchini can be delicious.

Two 4-ounce cans diced green chiles
6 large zucchini, sliced ¼-inch thick
Salt and pepper
8 ounces cheddar cheese, grated (2 cups)
2 eggs
²/₃ cup Bisquick
1¹/₂ cups milk
2 teaspoons dried crumbled oregano

Grease a 2-quart baking dish. Spread a layer of one-half of the chiles and then one-half of the zucchini in the dish. Sprinkle with salt and pepper, and add a layer of one-half of the cheese. Repeat the layers. In a medium bowl, combine the eggs, Bisquick, milk, and oregano. Mix well, and pour over the layers. Cover and refrigerate for several hours or overnight.

LATER

Preheat the oven to 350°F. Bake the casserole, covered, for $1\frac{1}{2}$ hours.

Serves 6

✴ Baked Zucchini

In late summer, our friends with gardens suddenly seem to have wheelbarrows full of zucchini on their hands. This recipe is a great use for surplus (and good for any other time of year, of course).

3 pounds medium zucchini, grated or finely chopped (peels left on)
1 medium yellow onion, grated or finely chopped
$\frac{1}{2}$ cup finely chopped parsley
3 or 4 tablespoons Bisquick
Salt and pepper
3 eggs, lightly beaten
8 ounces cheddar cheese, grated (2 cups)
2 tablespoons butter
Paprika

Grease a 9 x 13-inch baking dish, and set aside. In a large bowl, combine the zucchini, onion, parsley, and Bisquick. Season with salt and pepper to taste. Add the eggs and mix well. Transfer to the prepared baking dish. Spread the cheese on top, dot with the butter, and sprinkle with paprika. Refrigerate, covered, for up to 24 hours.

LATER

Preheat the oven to 350°F. Bake the casserole, uncovered, for 40 minutes.

Serves 4 to 6

Gingered Cucumbers

You'll find this unique dish will draw all kinds of compliments.

    2 medium cucumbers
    2 teaspoons salt
    2 teaspoons toasted sesame seeds
    1/2 cup rice vinegar
    5 tablespoons sugar
    2 tablespoons grated fresh ginger

NOW

Score the cucumber peels by running the tines of a fork down them lengthwise. Cut the cucumbers in half lengthwise, remove and discard the seeds, and thinly slice. Combine the cucumbers and salt in a medium bowl, mix well, and allow to sit for 5 minutes. Drain the cucumbers, squeeze out any excess liquid, and set aside.

In a small skillet over medium heat, toast the sesame seeds until lightly browned. Add the vinegar, sugar, and ginger, and bring to a boil. Pour the vinegar mixture over the cucumbers, and let it cool. Cover and refrigerate for 3 hours up to 2 days.

LATER
Serve cold, like pickles!

Serves 8

MAKE IT NOW, BAKE IT LATER!

Grand Finales

Whether you're on Broadway or in the kitchen, you can win big-time with the last act. And unlike every other part of your meal, the dessert can be completely independent of everything that came before it. The dessert can be a departure—a total surprise! And better still, as you can see from our recipes, the grand finale can be prepared completely in advance.

Your dessert selection should be decided, in part, by how you would like your dinner or event to be remembered. Do you need an elegant finish? Try Frozen Lemon Soufflé Cake (page 257). Do you just need a flat-out delicious cake for an intimate gathering? Try Chocolate Mousse Cake (page 262). The weather also plays a key role in picking a dessert. For those days when you're looking to beat the heat, try Delectable Dippers (page 273). And, of course, what's better than cookies for coffee dates, light lunches, or just for snacks?

Luckily, it's hard to go wrong with desserts. Here's an array of make-ahead grand finales that will delight you and your guests at any occasion or time of year.

✳ Butterscotch Toffee Heavenly Delight

How can you go wrong with a name like that? This was one of Mother's favorite desserts. Today, we like to use Skor brand English toffee bits rather than crush our own toffee.

1½ cups heavy cream
¾ cup butterscotch topping
½ teaspoon vanilla extract
1 store-bought angel food cake (about 1 pound)
One 10-ounce bag English toffee bits

NOW

In a medium bowl, whip the cream with an electric mixer until it starts to thicken. Slowly add the butterscotch and vanilla, and continue beating until thick. Using a long, serrated knife, cut the angel food cake into three layers horizontally. Spread about one-fourth of the butterscotch frosting between the layers, and sprinkle the layers generously with about one-fourth of the toffee chips.

Put the cake back together again, and frost the top and sides with the remaining butterscotch frosting. Sprinkle with the remaining toffee chips. Carefully cover the cake, and refrigerate for a minimum of 6 hours and up to 3 days.

LATER

Serve cold, immediately after removing from the refrigerator.

Serves 12

Frozen Lemon Soufflé Cake

This is a fantastic dessert to have on reserve in the freezer for unexpected company.

NOW
One 6-ounce package ladyfingers
One 28-ounce can sweetened condensed milk
8 eggs, separated
1 tablespoon lemon zest
3/4 cup lemon juice
1/4 teaspoon cream of tartar

LATER
2 tablespoons confectioners' sugar

NOW

Preheat the oven to 375°F. Lightly grease a 9-inch springform pan. Cover the entire bottom of the pan with ladyfingers, cutting them to fit as necessary. Stand the remaining ladyfingers around the sides of the pan, flat-side inward. Make sure the tops of the ladyfingers are even with the top of the pan. (You will have extra ladyfingers.) In a large bowl, combine the condensed milk, egg yolks, lemon zest, and lemon juice. Mix well, and set aside.

In a medium bowl, beat the egg whites with the cream of tartar until stiff. Gently fold the egg whites into the lemon mixture, stirring just until well combined. Pour on top of the ladyfingers, smoothing the top with a rubber spatula. Bake the cake for 25 minutes, until the top is lightly browned. Allow it to cool completely. Cover and freeze for up to 3 months.

Remove the outside ring of the pan. Dust the top of cake with the confectioners' sugar. Let it stand at room temperature for 15 to 20 minutes before serving. Leftovers may be refrigerated for 3 days more, or refrozen immediately for up to 3 months.

Serves 8 to 10

Cherry Berry Cloud

This truly is one of the best dessert recipes we have! Don't be put off by the many steps—this is really very easy and incredibly delicious. All you have to do is plan ahead.

NOW
6 egg whites
1/4 teaspoon salt
1/2 teaspoon cream of tartar
1 3/4 cups sugar

LATER I:
1 cup cream cheese (8 ounces), softened
1/2 cup sugar
1 teaspoon vanilla extract
2 cups heavy cream, whipped
3 cups miniature marshmallows

LATER II:

One 21-ounce can cherry pie filling
1 teaspoon lemon juice
2 tablespoons dark brown sugar
1 teaspoon almond extract, optional
2 cups sliced strawberries
Whipped cream, optional

NOW

Preheat the oven to 275°F. Grease a 9 x 13-inch baking dish, and set aside. In a medium bowl, beat the egg whites, salt, and cream of tartar with an electric mixer until foamy. Gradually add the sugar, beating until the mixture is stiff. Evenly spread the egg white mixture in the bottom of the baking dish, and bake for 1 hour. Turn off the oven, and let the dish sit in the oven for 8 to 12 hours more. Do not open the door. (We do this just before we go to bed.)

LATER I

In a medium bowl, combine the cream cheese, sugar, and vanilla, beating until smooth. Fold in the whipped cream and marshmallows. Spread over the egg white base. Cover and refrigerate for 24 hours. (We do this when we wake up!)

LATER II

In a medium bowl, combine the cherry pie filling, lemon juice, brown sugar, almond extract, and strawberries, and mix well. Cut the chilled base into squares. Spoon the cherry-berry topping over each square. You may top with additional whipped cream if desired.

TIP For the Fourth of July, sprinkle some fresh blueberries on each square.

Serves 12 to 15

Chocolate Trifle

Need we say more!

> 1 box chocolate cake mix (about 18¼ ounces)
> 2 packages (each 4-serving size) chocolate instant pudding
> 2 cups crushed chocolate cookie crumbs
> One 16-ounce tub frozen nondairy whipped topping, thawed, or 2 pints
>   heavy cream, whipped
> One 10-ounce bag English toffee bits
> 2 cups chopped walnuts or pecans, or toasted sliced almonds, optional

NOW

Prepare the chocolate cake according to the package directions, and bake in a 9 x 13-inch baking dish. Allow the cake to cool, crumble it, and set aside. Prepare the chocolate pudding according to the package directions, and set aside.

In a large decorative glass bowl, spread a thin layer of crumbled chocolate cake; then a layer of cookie crumbs; then a layer of pudding; next a layer of whipped cream; and sprinkle with toffee bits and nuts. Repeat the layers until your bowl is full. (You may have extras.) Make sure to spread all the ingredients to the edge of the bowl so the layers will show through the glass. Cover and refrigerate for several hours or up to 3 days.

LATER

Present the spectacular glass bowl to your guests before serving cold.

Serves 10 to 12

✳ Chocolate-Mint Angel Cake

This one's a dazzler.

>1 store-bought angel food cake (about 1 pound)
>1 quart heavy cream
>1 cup sugar
>$^1/_3$ cup cocoa powder
>1 dash of salt
>1 teaspoon peppermint extract, optional
>$^1/_2$ cup slivered almonds
>1 tablespoon butter
>1 ounce bittersweet chocolate

N O W

Using a long serrated knife, cut the angel food cake into four layers, horizontally, and set aside. In a large bowl, combine the cream, sugar, cocoa powder, and salt. Add the peppermint extract, if desired, and mix well. Cover and refrigerate for 1 hour. Then whip until the cream holds soft peaks.

Spread about one-fourth of the whipped cream mixture between each layer of the angel food cake, as you would spread icing on a layer cake. Ice the top and sides of the layered cake with the remaining whipped cream mixture, and set aside. In a small skillet over medium heat, toast the almonds in the butter until they turn golden brown. Transfer the almonds to paper towels to drain. Grate the chocolate on top of the iced cake. Sprinkle the almonds on top. Cover and refrigerate overnight.

LATER
Serve the cake cold.

⌐→ **TIP** You can use a regular-sized Hershey's milk chocolate bar instead of the bitter-sweet chocolate.

Serves 10 generously and 12 easily

Chocolate Mousse Cake

This is a scrumptious grand finale to have waiting in the freezer for the end of your next family dinner or dinner party.

NOW
One 12-ounce bag semisweet chocolate chips
3 tablespoons confectioners' sugar
3 tablespoons water
7 egg yolks, lightly beaten *(see the Note on page 86 about the use of raw eggs)*
7 egg whites, beaten until they form peaks
One 6-ounce package ladyfingers

LATER
One 8-ounce tub frozen nondairy whipped topping, thawed, or 1 cup
   heavy cream, whipped
Shaved chocolate or cocoa powder, optional

Line the sides and bottom of a 9 x 5-inch loaf pan with plastic wrap, and set aside. In the top of a double boiler, melt the chocolate chips, and stir until smooth. Add the confectioners' sugar and water, mix well, and remove from heat. Add the egg yolks, whisking to incorporate them quickly. Let the chocolate mixture sit for about 15 minutes. Test the temperature, and when cool, fold in the egg whites. Mix well.

Make a layer of the ladyfingers in the bottom of the plastic-lined loaf pan. Cover with a layer of chocolate mousse. Repeat layers, ending with ladyfingers. Cover well and freeze for at least 2 days or up to 3 months.

LATER

Twelve hours before serving, transfer the mousse cake from the freezer to the refrigerator. When the cake has thawed, invert it onto a serving plate and remove the plastic wrap. Ice the entire cake with the whipped topping. If desired, decorate the top of the cake with shaved chocolate or a light sprinkling of cocoa powder. Serve cold.

Serves 6 to 8

Chocolate Éclair Cake

This cake is just like one big, fancy s'more.

2 boxes (4-serving size each) instant French vanilla pudding
2 cups plus 3 tablespoons milk, divided
One 12-ounce tub frozen nondairy whipped topping, thawed
One 14-ounce box whole graham crackers
$1/3$ cup cocoa powder
2 tablespoons butter, softened
2 tablespoons light corn syrup
1 teaspoon vanilla extract
$1^1/_2$ cup confectioners' sugar

NOW

In a medium bowl, combine the pudding mix with 2 cups of the milk. Mix well, and let it sit for 5 minutes. Fold in the whipped topping. In a 9 x 13-inch baking dish, spread a layer of one-third of the whole graham crackers. Top with one-half of the pudding mixture. Repeat, ending with a third layer of graham crackers. Set aside.

In a medium bowl, make the chocolate icing by combining the cocoa powder, butter, corn syrup, vanilla, confectioners' sugar, and the remaining 3 tablespoons milk. Beat with an electric mixer until smooth, and spread the icing on top of the graham cracker layer. Refrigerate the cake for at least 1 day or up to 3 days.

LATER

Cut the cake into squares and serve cold.

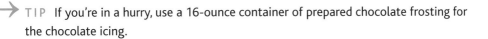

TIP If you're in a hurry, use a 16-ounce container of prepared chocolate frosting for the chocolate icing.

Serves 12 to 15

New York Cheesecake

This recipe was given to us years ago by a friend from New York. It may be our all-time favorite cheesecake!

Crust
1¹/₂ cups graham cracker crumbs
5 tablespoons sugar
¹/₄ cup butter (¹/₂ stick), melted
1 teaspoon cinnamon, optional
¹/₂ teaspoon nutmeg, optional
¹/₂ teaspoon ginger, optional

Cheesecake
5 eggs
4 cups cream cheese (32 ounces)
4 cups sour cream
1¹/₂ cups sugar
1 tablespoon vanilla extract
1 teaspoon almond extract

NOW

To make the crust, grease a 9-inch springform pan, and set aside. Combine the crumbs, sugar, and melted butter. If desired, add the cinnamon, nutmeg, and ginger, and mix well. Press into the prepared pan to form a crust, and set aside.

To make the cheesecake, remove the eggs, cream cheese, and sour cream from the refrigerator, and let sit up to 1 hour to come to room temperature.

Preheat the oven to 350°F. In a small bowl, beat the eggs until they are foamy, and set aside. In a medium bowl, combine the cream cheese and sour cream, beating with an electric mixer until smooth. Add the sugar, vanilla, almond extract, and eggs, and beat until smooth. Pour the cheesecake filling over the crust, and bake the cake for 1 hour. Turn off the oven, and let the cheesecake remain in the oven for 1 hour more. (Do not open the oven door.) Remove the cake from the oven, and allow it to cool completely. Cover and refrigerate until thoroughly chilled, at least 4 hours or up to 2 weeks.

 LATER
Serve cold.

 TIP Serve this cake in small wedges, either plain or with your favorite topping. As for toppings, we like fresh strawberries, fresh raspberries, or cherry or blueberry pie filling.

Serves 12 to 15

Surprise Pudding Cake

This is great for a fun change of pace. The "surprise" is the Ritz cracker crust, which is decidedly unusual.

NOW
56 Ritz crackers (approximately 2 rolls), crushed
1 cup butter (2 sticks), melted
2 packages (4-serving size each) pistachio-flavored instant pudding
1⅓ cups milk
1 quart vanilla ice cream, softened
One 8-ounce tub frozen nondairy whipped topping, thawed

LATER
15 maraschino cherries, or two 10½-ounce cans cherry pie filling mixed
   with 1 teaspoon vanilla extract and 2 tablespoons brown sugar

NOW
Preheat the oven to 350°F. Lightly grease a 9 x 13-inch baking dish. In a large bowl, combine the crushed crackers and melted butter. Mix well, and press into the bottom of the prepared baking dish. Bake the crust for 10 minutes and set aside to cool.

In a large bowl, combine the pudding mix and milk. Beat in the ice cream with an electric mixer, and spread the mixture over the cooled crust. Ice the cake with the whipped topping. Cover and freeze for up to 3 months.

LATER
Remove the cake from the freezer, and let it sit for about 30 minutes. Top each serving with a cherry or with the cherry pie filling mixture.

Serves 15

Strawberry Angel Dessert

So easy to make, this dessert really keeps summer alive if you serve it throughout the year.

One 6-ounce package strawberry Jell-O
2 cups boiling water
One 32-ounce package frozen sliced strawberries, partially thawed
One 12-ounce tub frozen nondairy whipped topping, thawed
1 store-bought angel food cake (about 1 pound), torn into bite-sized
    pieces

NOW

In a medium bowl, dissolve the Jell-O in the boiling water. Add the strawberries, and mix well. Refrigerate until the Jell-O begins to thicken, 35 to 45 minutes. Add the whipped topping and mix thoroughly.

In a 9 x 13-inch baking dish, layer one-half the strawberry mixture, top with a layer of the cake pieces, and then the remaining strawberry mixture. Cover and refrigerate for 4 hours or up to 3 days.

LATER

Serve in ice cream dishes.

Serves 8 to 10

Turtle Cake

This cake has all our favorite flavors rolled into one dessert: chocolate, caramel, toffee, and pecans.

1 box chocolate cake mix (about 18$^1/_4$ ounces)
One 12-ounce jar dulce de leche sauce or caramel sauce
One 8-ounce tub frozen nondairy whipped topping, thawed
1 cup English toffee bits
$^1/_2$ cup chopped pecans

NOW

Prepare the chocolate cake according to the package directions, and bake it in a 9 x 13-inch baking dish. Remove the cake from the oven, and while it's still warm, take the end of a wooden spoon and poke holes all over the cake, all the way through to the bottom of the dish. Pour the caramel sauce all over the top of the cake, and let it ooze down into the holes. Allow the caramel to cool completely. When cool, ice with the whipped topping and sprinkle with the toffee bits and pecans. Cover and refrigerate for several hours or overnight.

LATER

Serve cold or at room temperature.

Serves 12 to 15

Eggnog Mousse

Thanks to the bourbon, this molded dessert has the true flavor of holiday eggnog. For a milder flavor, you can substitute rum for the bourbon.

NOW

One $1/2$-ounce package unflavored gelatin

1 cup cold water

8 egg yolks *(see the Note on page 86 about the use of raw eggs)*

$3/4$ cup good bourbon

$1/4$ teaspoon salt

8 egg whites

1 cup sugar

1 cup heavy cream, whipped

LATER

Optional toppings

Nondairy whipped topping or sweetened whipped cream

Toasted slivered almonds

Grated nutmeg

NOW

In a medium saucepan over medium heat, combine the gelatin and cold water. Cook, stirring constantly, until the gelatin has dissolved. Remove from heat, and set aside. In a medium bowl, beat the egg yolks with an electric mixer until thick and creamy. Add the bourbon, and mix well. Add the gelatin, and blend thoroughly. Cover and refrigerate, whisking occasionally, until slightly thickened, about 20 minutes.

In a medium bowl, combine the salt and egg whites, beating with an electric mixer until they start taking shape. Gradually add the sugar, and beat until the egg whites are smooth, shiny, and hold a peak. Whisk one-third of the egg white mixture into the gelatin mixture, and set aside. Fold the whipped cream into the remaining egg white mixture. Gently add the gelatin mixture, and fold together until thoroughly combined. Pour the mousse into a serving bowl. Cover and refrigerate for 2 hours or overnight.

LATER

Serve cold in sherbet dishes. If desired, decorate the top of each serving with a dollop of whipped topping, the almonds, and a sprinkle of nutmeg.

Serves 8

Fresh Strawberries and Dips

We love to serve a large basket of fresh strawberries with several different dips. Just wash the berries and let them dry—don't even cap them!

NOW

Simple Sugar Dip
¹/₂ cup confectioners' sugar
¹/₄ cup firmly packed dark brown sugar

Orange Dip
1 cup heavy cream, whipped to soft peaks with 1 tablespoon confectioners'
    sugar; or one 8-ounce tub frozen nondairy whipped topping, thawed
2 tablespoons frozen orange juice concentrate, thawed, or Grand Marnier
1 tablespoon grated orange zest

Brown Sugar Dip
1 cup sour cream
$^1/_4$ cup firmly packed dark brown sugar
1 tablespoon rum, optional

Maple Dip
1 cup sour cream
$^1/_4$ cup maple syrup
$^1/_2$ teaspoon nutmeg

LATER
2 quarts fresh strawberries

NOW

To make the Simple Sugar Dip, combine the sugars in a small bowl. Transfer to an airtight container, where they will keep indefinitely.

To make the Orange Dip, stir all the ingredients together in a small bowl. Cover and refrigerate for up to 2 days.

To make the Brown Sugar Dip, combine all the ingredients, including the rum if desired, in a small bowl. Mix well, cover, and refrigerate for up to 2 days.

To make the Maple Dip, combine all the ingredients in a small bowl. Mix well, cover, and refrigerate for up to 2 days.

LATER

Mix each of the dips thoroughly before serving. Serve the dips in individual dishes alongside the strawberries.

→ TIP You can also serve any of these dips with the Delectable Dippers, below.

Serves 8 to 10

Delectable Dippers

Our family and friends simply love this fresh fruit dessert! It's the perfect ending to a great meal.

NOW
Ambrosia Dip
1 cup cream cheese (8 ounces), softened
One 14-ounce can sweetened condensed milk
One 8-ounce tub frozen nondairy whipped topping, thawed

LATER
Chocolate Fondue
4 ounces unsweetened chocolate
$1/2$ cup butter (1 stick)
1 cup half-and-half
$1^1/2$ cups sugar
$1/8$ teaspoon salt
2 teaspoons vanilla extract

A variety of the following

2 cups bite-sized pieces of cantaloupe or other melon

2 cups bite-sized pieces of pineapple

2 cups small strawberries

2 cups grapes

2 cups 1-inch pieces of banana, coated with lemon or pineapple juice

4 cups bite-sized pieces of angel food or pound cake

NOW

To make the Ambrosia Dip, combine the cream cheese and condensed milk in a medium bowl, mixing until smooth. Fold in the whipped topping. Put in a serving bowl, cover, and refrigerate for up to 3 days.

LATER

Stir the Ambrosia Dip well before serving.

To make the Chocolate Fondue, melt the chocolate and butter in a medium saucepan over low heat. Mix in the half-and-half, sugar, salt, and vanilla. Cook, stirring frequently, until thickened. Remove the fondue from the heat, and transfer it to a serving bowl.

Serve the two dips with a selection of the fruit and cake—the more choices the better!

Serves 12

Snickerdoodles

These are our daughter Amy's favorite cookies.

NOW
2³/₄ cups all-purpose flour
2 teaspoons cream of tartar
1 teaspoon baking soda
¹/₂ teaspoon salt
1 cup butter (2 sticks), softened
1¹/₂ cups sugar
2 eggs
1 teaspoon vanilla extract

LATER
2 teaspoons cinnamon
3 tablespoons sugar

NOW

In a medium bowl, combine the flour, cream of tartar, baking soda, and salt, and mix well. In a large bowl, combine the butter and sugar, beating with an electric mixer until smooth. Add the eggs, one at a time, mixing well after each. Add the vanilla and mix well. Add the flour mixture, one-third at a time, mixing well after each addition. Cover and refrigerate for 1 hour or up to 1 week.

LATER

Preheat the oven to 400°F. In a small bowl, combine the cinnamon and sugar, and set aside. Roll the dough into balls the size of small walnuts and then roll them in the cinnamon mixture. Place the coated balls on an ungreased baking sheet, about 2 inches apart. Bake for 8 to 10 minutes, until lightly browned. (The cookies will puff up and then flatten out with a crinkled top.)

TIP Since the dough will keep in the refrigerator for up to 1 week, you can bake a few cookies at a time or bake them all at once.

Makes 5 to 6 dozen cookies

✳ Christmas Cookies

These are truly a Goodfellow tradition! Every Christmas when they were young, Scott and his sister, Jane, would each invite a friend over to decorate these cookies. Now our children do the same.

NOW
6 cups all-purpose flour
1 teaspoon salt
2 cups butter (4 sticks), softened (no substitutions, please!)
2 cups sugar
4 eggs
2 teaspoons vanilla extract

LATER
4 egg whites *(see the Note on page 86 about the use of raw eggs)*
$1/2$ teaspoon cream of tartar

$^1/_2$ teaspoon vanilla extract
5 cups sifted confectioners' sugar
Food coloring
A selection of candy and cake decorations

NOW

In a medium bowl, combine the flour and salt, and set aside. In a large bowl, beat the butter with an electric mixer until soft and smooth. Gradually add the sugar, mixing well, and blend until the mixture is light and fluffy. Add the eggs and vanilla, and mix well. (The dough may become lumpy, but keep mixing it until the lumps are small.) Add the flour mixture a little at a time, and mix well after each addition. Cover well and refrigerate for at least 5 hours or up to 1 week.

LATER

Preheat the oven to 375°F. Flour a rolling pin and a work surface well. Take a small portion of dough and roll it to $^1/_8$-inch thickness. Cut out shapes with cookie cutters, dipping them in flour before each cut. Carefully transfer the shapes to ungreased baking sheets, and bake the cookies for about 10 minutes, until the edges are light brown. Carefully transfer the baked cookies to sheets of waxed paper to cool. When cool, frost as described below.

Now comes the fun!

In a medium bowl, combine the egg whites, cream of tartar, and vanilla, beating with an electric mixer until foamy. Gradually beat in the confectioners' sugar until the frosting stands in firm peaks. Divide the frosting among 5 custard or coffee cups. Tint 4 of the cups with food coloring—red, blue, yellow, and green. Make your colors bright! The fifth cup of frosting is white.

Now you are ready to give each cookie a complete color job!

Spread the frosting on the cookies using a separate knife for each color. (If the frosting hardens, stir in a few drops of hot water.) Keep several bottles of cake decorations nearby, and use them on the cookies as you wish.

TIP This recipe halves easily. The dough will keep for 1 week in the refrigerator, so you can make as many cookies as you want at a time. If you don't have time or don't want to frost your cookies, sprinkle them with colored sugar, sprinkles, or cinnamon red hots before baking.

Makes 70 to 90 cookies, depending on the size of your cookie cutters

✳ Washington Cookies

Our daughter Allison's favorite cookies. Mother always had them ready for our arrival when we would go visit her.

1¹/₂ cups all-purpose flour
1 teaspoon baking soda
1 teaspoon salt
1 cup margarine (2 sticks)
³/₄ cup firmly packed brown sugar
³/₄ cup sugar
2 eggs
1 teaspoon vanilla extract
1 cup chopped pecans or walnuts
2 cups rolled oats
1 cup chocolate chips

NOW

Preheat the oven to 350°F. Grease a baking sheet, and set aside. In a small bowl, combine the flour, baking soda, and salt, and set aside. In a medium bowl, combine the margarine, brown sugar, and sugar, beating with an electric mixer until light and fluffy. Add the eggs, and beat well to combine. Add the vanilla, and mix well. Stir in the flour mixture. Add the pecans, oats, and chocolate chips, and mix well.

Roll the dough into balls the size of small walnuts and place them about 2 inches apart on the prepared baking sheet. Bake for 10 to 12 minutes, until light brown. Allow the cookies to cool thoroughly, and freeze them for up to 3 months.

LATER
Let the cookies sit at room temperature overnight before serving.

Makes about 6 dozen cookies

Firemen's Fudge

This recipe was given to Mother by one of our local firemen years ago and we have been making it ever since. Trust me, everyone *will want to learn your fudge-making secret!*

> One 12-ounce bag vanilla milk chips
> 1 cup crushed cocktail peanuts
> 1 cup crushed (but not powdery) pretzels

NOW
Spray a baking sheet with vegetable cooking spray, and set aside. Spray the inside of the top of a double boiler lightly with vegetable cooking spray. Melt the vanilla chips in the prepared double boiler. As soon as the chips have melted, toss in the pretzels and peanuts. Stir rapidly to combine, and pour onto the prepared baking sheet. Spread the candy mixture as thinly as possible. Put the baking sheet in the freezer for at least 1 hour, and when the candy is thoroughly frozen, crack it with the back of a spoon into bite-sized pieces. Transfer to an airtight container, and keep frozen for up to 3 months.

Put the fudge in a serving dish and watch it disappear! It does not have to be refrigerated again. Serve cold or at room temperature.

⤷ TIP You can use 1 cup crushed candy canes instead of the peanuts and pretzels.

Makes about 3 cups candy

Twinkie Pie

This will bring back many childhood memories, especially if you were a Twinkie lover.

8 to 10 Twinkies
One 21-ounce can cherry pie filling
2 boxes (4-serving size each) instant vanilla pudding
2¹/₂ cups milk
3 medium bananas, sliced
One 8-ounce tub frozen nondairy whipped topping, thawed
¹/₂ cup chopped pecans

NOW
Split the Twinkies lengthwise, and line the bottom of a 9 x 13-inch baking dish with the Twinkie halves, cut side up. Pour the cherry pie filling over the Twinkies, and set aside. In a medium bowl, combine the pudding and

milk, stir until stiff, and spread over the cherries. Spread the banana slices over the pudding. Spread the whipped topping over the banana slices, and sprinkle the pecans on top. Cover and refrigerate for 3 hours or overnight.

LATER
Serve cold, scooping the pie out with a spoon.

TIP You can use blueberry pie filling or lemon pudding instead of the cherry pie filling.

Serves 10 to 12

Mayflower Pumpkin Pie

Mother served this pumpkin pie at Thanksgiving. It was always our first choice for dessert!

NOW
One 15-ounce can pumpkin
1^1/$_2$ cups sugar
^{1}/$_2$ teaspoon salt
2 teaspoons pumpkin pie spice
1 teaspoon vanilla extract
1 pint vanilla ice cream, softened
One 9-inch prebaked pie shell

LATER

One 8-ounce tub frozen nondairy whipped topping, thawed, or 2 cups
heavy cream, whipped

NOW

In a medium bowl, combine the pumpkin, sugar, salt, pumpkin pie spice, and vanilla. Mix well, and beat in the ice cream with an electric mixer. Pour the pumpkin filling into the pie shell, and freeze for about 1 hour. Cover and return to the freezer for up to 3 months.

LATER

Serve with a generous dollop of the whipped cream on each serving.

TIP Mother used a regular prebaked pie shell, but we prefer a gingersnap or graham cracker crust.

Serves 6 to 8

Sleepy Hollow Pumpkin Dip

Everyone loves this delicious dessert dip. It easily doubles as a special gift from the kitchen—just put the dip in half-pint jars and tie a colorful ribbon around the top of each.

NOW
2 cups confectioners' sugar
1 cup cream cheese (8 ounces), softened
2 cups canned pumpkin pie filling
2 teaspoons pumpkin pie spice

LATER
Gingersnaps

NOW

In a large mixing bowl, combine the confectioners' sugar and cream cheese, beating with an electric mixer until well blended. Beat in the pumpkin pie filling and pumpkin pie spice. Transfer to an airtight container, and refrigerate for up to 2 weeks.

LATER

Serve cold, with gingersnaps for dipping.

TIP If you cannot find pumpkin pie filling, use a 15-ounce can of pumpkin and mix it with 1 tablespoon pumpkin pie spice.

Makes 2 cups

Lemonade Pie

This is very refreshing and extremely easy to prepare.

One 6-ounce can frozen pink lemonade concentrate, thawed
One 14-ounce can sweetened condensed milk
One 8-ounce tub frozen nondairy whipped topping, thawed
One 9-inch graham cracker pie crust

NOW

In a medium bowl, combine the lemonade and condensed milk, and mix
well. Fold in the whipped topping. Pour the filling into the pie crust.
Refrigerate for 4 hours or overnight.

LATER

Serve the pie cold.

Serves 6 to 8

Fresh Peach Pie

No one will guess how you made this nutty crust, Ann's favorite!

3 egg whites
1 cup sugar
14 saltine crackers, crushed
1 teaspoon vanilla extract
$^1/_2$ teaspoon baking powder
$^1/_2$ cup chopped pecans
4 to 5 fresh, ripe peaches, peeled and sliced
One 12-ounce tub frozen nondairy whipped topping, thawed

NOW

Preheat the oven to 325°F. Grease a 9-inch pie dish, and set aside. Beat the egg whites with an electric mixer until foamy. Then, gradually beat in the sugar. Keep beating until the mixture holds soft peaks. Add the crackers, vanilla, and baking powder, and mix well. Sprinkle the pecans in the bottom of the prepared pie dish. Pour the egg white mixture on top. Bake the crust for 30 minutes. (It will puff up and crack. Don't worry.) Allow it to cool.

Arrange the peach slices on the crust in the pie dish. (Sprinkle with a little sugar if the peaches are too sour.) Cover the entire pie with the whipped topping, making sure to seal the edges with the topping to keep the peaches from turning brown. Refrigerate for several hours or up to 2 days.

LATER

Serve the pie cold.

TIP For a nice presentation, sprinkle pumpkin pie spice or nutmeg on top of the whipped topping. Also, you can try making this pie with other kinds of fruit, such as strawberries.

Serves 6 to 8

Ice Cream Toppings

Ice cream has always been one of our family's favorite desserts. Here are two wonderful toppings that will make your ice cream even more special.

NOW
Praline Sundae

$^{1}/_{4}$ cup butter or margarine ($^{1}/_{2}$ stick)

1$^{1}/_{4}$ cups firmly packed dark brown sugar

16 large marshmallows

2 tablespoons light corn syrup

1 dash of salt

1 cup evaporated milk

$^{1}/_{2}$ cup chopped pecans, toasted in a dry skillet over high heat

1 teaspoon vanilla extract

Chocolate Sauce

1 cup sugar

2 tablespoons cocoa powder

One 5-ounce can Carnation evaporated milk (no substitutions, please!)

2 tablespoons butter

1 teaspoon vanilla extract

LATER

Ice cream

NOW

To make the Praline Sundae, melt the butter in a medium saucepan over low heat. Add the brown sugar, marshmallows, corn syrup, and salt. Cook, stirring frequently, until the marshmallows have melted and the mixture comes to a boil. Boil for 1 minute, then remove from heat and allow the mixture to cool for 5 minutes. Stir in the evaporated milk, pecans, and vanilla. Transfer to an airtight container, and refrigerate for up to 2 weeks.

To make the Chocolate Sauce, in a medium saucepan over low heat, combine the sugar and cocoa, and cook, stirring frequently, for 2 minutes. Add the evaporated milk and butter, and bring to a boil for 2 minutes, stirring constantly. Remove from heat, and add the vanilla. Allow the sauce to cool. Transfer to an airtight container, and refrigerate for up to 2 weeks.

LATER

Serve sauce warm or cold over your favorite flavors of ice cream.

Makes 1 1/2 to 2 cups of each topping

Heavenly Ice Cream Dessert

Willy Wonka never had it so good! This is great to have in the freezer any time of the year—it's saved us more than once when people have dropped by unexpectedly.

24 chocolate cream sandwich cookies, crushed
$^{1}/_{2}$ cup butter (1 stick), melted
$^{1}/_{2}$ gallon chocolate chip ice cream (or your favorite flavor), softened
3 ounces unsweetened chocolate
2 tablespoons butter
1 cup sugar
1 dash of salt
One 10-ounce can evaporated milk
$^{1}/_{2}$ teaspoon vanilla extract
2 cups heavy cream, whipped and sweetened to taste
$^{1}/_{2}$ to 1 cup chopped nuts or English toffee bits

NOW

Butter a 9 x 13-inch freezer-safe dish, and set aside. In a medium bowl, combine the crushed cookies and butter, and mix well. Press the cookie crumb crust into the bottom of the prepared dish, and freeze for 20 to 30 minutes. Once frozen, spread a layer of the ice cream on top of the crust, and freeze for about 20 minutes more.

In a medium saucepan over low heat, melt the chocolate and butter together. Add the sugar, salt, and evaporated milk. Bring to boil, stirring until it has thickened, about 5 minutes. Remove from heat, and add the vanilla. Chill the chocolate mixture until cool, then spread it on top of the ice cream layer. Freeze again for about 1 hour.

Spread the whipped cream over the chocolate layer, and sprinkle the chopped nuts on top. Freeze overnight, or until thoroughly frozen, then cover well, and return to the freezer for up to 3 months.

LATER
Cut into squares and serve cold on plates.

TIP At Christmastime, use peppermint stick ice cream, omit the nuts, and top with crushed candy canes. Or make a Tin Roof Sundae by sprinkling 1 cup crushed peanuts over the chocolate layer before freezing it. You can do almost anything your imagination comes up with!

Serves 15

MAKE IT NOW, BAKE IT LATER!

Aloha Dessert

Eat this and you'll think you're in the tropics. We like the lime sherbet best, but it's also delicious with pineapple or any other flavor.

One 13-ounce package hard coconut macaroons, crushed
One 6-ounce container macadamia nut pieces
$^1/_4$ cup butter ($^1/_2$ stick), melted
$^1/_2$ gallon lime sherbet, softened
One 12-ounce tub frozen nondairy whipped topping, thawed

NOW

Lightly grease a 9 x 13-inch freezer-safe dish, and set aside. Reserve 1 cup of the crushed cookies and 1 cup of the nuts to top the dessert. In a medium bowl, combine the remaining crushed cookies with the melted butter. Mix well, and press into the prepared dish to form a crust. Sprinkle the remaining nuts on top, and freeze for 20 minutes. In a medium bowl, combine the sherbet with the whipped topping. Spread this sherbet mixture on top of the cookies and nuts. Sprinkle with the reserved cookie crumbs and nuts. Cover and freeze for up to 3 months.

LATER

Serve cold.

TIP If you spray vegetable cooking spray on the inside of any dish or container you plan to fill and freeze, the dessert will come out more easily later.

Serves 12 to 15

Sherbet Delight

This wonderful, refreshing dessert is an Easter tradition at our house.

NOW
2 cups heavy cream
2 tablespoons sugar
1 teaspoon vanilla extract
12 soft macaroon cookies, crumbled
1 cup chopped pecans
1 quart orange sherbet (or your favorite flavor), softened

LATER
12 to 15 fresh mint leaves, optional
12 to 15 maraschino cherries, optional

NOW

Lightly spray a 9 x 13-inch freezer-safe dish with vegetable cooking spray, and set aside. In a medium bowl, combine the cream, sugar, and vanilla, beating with an electric mixer to form whipped cream. Add the crumbled cookies and pecans, and mix well. Spread one-half of this mixture in the bottom of the prepared dish, reserving the rest.

Put in the freezer for about 20 minutes, until frozen. Gently spread the sherbet over the frozen whipped cream layer. Spread the reserved whipped cream mixture on top of the sherbet, and return it to the freezer. When thoroughly frozen, cover, and keep frozen for up to 3 months.

LATER

Cut into squares and serve cold. For a beautiful presentation, top each serving of sherbet with a mint leaf and a maraschino cherry.

TIP If you dip a knife in warm water before cutting a frozen dessert, it will slice much more easily.

Serves 12 to 15

Chocolate Chip Ice Cream Pie

Our nephew, Willie, thinks this is the best *dessert ever—it's crunchy, with lots of chocolate and ice cream!*

NOW
1 cup chocolate syrup
1 cup semisweet chocolate chips
2 cups crisp rice cereal
$^{1}/_{4}$ cup sour cream
1 quart chocolate chip ice cream (or your favorite flavor), softened

LATER
One 8-ounce tub frozen nondairy whipped topping, thawed
6 to 8 cherries

NOW

Spray a deep 9-inch pie dish with vegetable cooking spray, and set aside. In a small, microwave-safe bowl, combine the chocolate syrup and chocolate chips. Microwave on high (100 percent) power until hot, about 45 seconds. Stir until smooth. Reserve $^{1}/_{2}$ cup of this chocolate mixture.

In a medium bowl, combine the remaining chocolate mixture and the cereal. Mix well, and press into the bottom and sides of the prepared pie dish. Freeze until firm, about 15 minutes. In a small bowl, combine the reserved ½ cup chocolate mixture and the sour cream. Mix well and set aside.

Spread one-half of the ice cream in the prepared pie plate. Drizzle with the chocolate-sour cream mixture. Top with the remaining ice cream. Freeze the pie until firm, at least 1 hour. Then, cover, and keep in the freezer for up to 3 months.

LATER

Top each serving with a dollop of whipped topping and a cherry.

Serves 6 to 8

Chocolate Velvet Pie

This is a wonderful melt-in-your-mouth chocolate delight.

1¹/₂ cups chocolate wafer crumbs
¹/₃ cup butter (²/₃ stick), melted
1 cup cream cheese (8 ounces), softened
¹/₂ cup sugar, divided
1 teaspoon vanilla extract
2 egg yolks, well beaten *(see the Note on page 86 about the use of raw eggs)*
1 cup chocolate chips, melted
2 egg whites, beaten to form soft peaks
1 cup heavy cream, whipped
1 cup chopped pecans

NOW

Preheat the oven to 325°F. Lightly grease a 9-inch springform pan. In a medium bowl, combine the wafer crumbs and butter. Mix well, and press into the bottom of the springform pan to form a crust. Bake for 10 minutes.

In a medium bowl, combine the cream cheese, ¹/₄ cup of the sugar, and vanilla, beating until well blended. Add the egg yolks and melted chocolate, and mix well. In a small bowl, slowly beat the remaining ¹/₄ cup sugar into the egg whites just until well combined. Gently fold the egg white mixture into the chocolate mixture. Fold in the whipped cream, then the pecans. Pour over the baked crumbs, and freeze for at least 4 hours or up to 3 months.

LATER

Serve the pie cold.

Serves 8 to 10

Crunchy Ice Cream Pie

A great chilled dessert with a Southern accent.

NOW
1 cup flaked coconut
$1/2$ cup firmly packed dark brown sugar
3 cups crisp rice cereal
$1/2$ cup butter (1 stick), melted
1 cup chopped pecans
$1/2$ gallon butter pecan ice cream (or your favorite flavor), softened

LATER
2 tablespoons hot fudge or caramel sauce

NOW

Preheat the oven to 300°F. Spray a 9 x 13-inch baking dish or two pie pans with vegetable cooking spray, and set aside. In a medium bowl, combine the coconut, brown sugar, cereal, butter, and pecans, and mix well. Loosely spread the mixture on a baking sheet. Bake for 30 minutes, stirring every 15 minutes. Remove from the oven, and allow the cereal mixture to cool.

Spread one-half of the cereal mixture in the prepared baking dish, and press down firmly to form a crust. Top with the ice cream and then the remaining cereal mixture. Press the cereal mixture into the ice cream and freeze. When frozen, cover and return to the freezer for up to 3 months.

LATER

Serve with the hot fudge sauce drizzled on top.

Serves 12 to 15

Conversion Charts

WEIGHT EQUIVALENTS

The metric weights given in this chart are not exact equivalents, but have been rounded up or down slightly to make measuring easier.

AVOIRDUPOIS	METRIC
¼ oz	7 g
½ oz	15 g
1 oz	30 g
2 oz	60 g
3 oz	90 g
4 oz	115 g
5 oz	150 g
6 oz	175 g
7 oz	200 g
8 oz (½ lb)	225 g
9 oz	250 g
10 oz	300 g
11 oz	325 g
12 oz	350 g
13 oz	375 g
14 oz	400 g
15 oz	425 g
16 oz (1 lb)	450 g
1½ lb	750 g
2 lb	900 g
2¼ lb	1 kg
3 lb	1.4 kg
4 lb	1.8 kg

VOLUME EQUIVALENTS

These are not exact equivalents for American cups and spoons, but have been rounded up or down slightly to make measuring easier.

AMERICAN	METRIC	IMPERIAL
¼ t	1.2 ml	
½ t	2.5 ml	
1 t	5.0 ml	
½ T (1.5 t)	7.5 ml	
1 T (3 t)	15 ml	
¼ cup (4 T)	60 ml 2 fl oz	
⅓ cup (5 T)	75 ml 2½ fl oz	
½ cup (8 T)	125 ml	4 fl oz
⅔ cup (10 T)	150 ml	5 fl oz
¾ cup (12 T)	175 ml	6 fl oz
1 cup (16 T)	250 ml	8 fl oz
1¼ cups	300 ml	10 fl oz (½ pt)
1½ cups	350 ml	12 fl oz
2 cups (1 pint)	500 ml	16 fl oz
2½ cups	625 ml	20 fl oz (1 pint)
1 quart	1 liter 32 fl oz	

OVEN TEMPERATURE EQUIVALENTS

OVEN MARK	F	C	GAS
Very cool	250–275	130–140	½–1
Cool	300	150	2
Warm	325	170	3
Moderate	350	180	4
Moderately hot	375	190	5
	400	200	6
Hot	425	220	7
	450	230	8
Very hot	475	250	9

Index